How to Buy Land

L. John Wachtel

Sterling Publishing Co., Inc.   New York

Library of Congress Cataloging in Publication Data
Wachtel, L. John.
　How to buy land.

　Bibliography: p.
　Includes index.
　1. Real property—United States—Purchasing.
2. Land titles—Registration and transfer—
United States.　3. Real estate investment—
United States.　I. Title.
HD255.W25　　333.33'02'02　　81-85032
ISBN 0-8069-7156-8　　AACR2
ISBN 0-8069-7157-6 (lib. bdg.)
ISBN 0-8069-7602-0 (pbk.)

CONTENTS

This book is dedicated to the memory of Russel E. Uhland, a father when I had no other, a teacher, a mentor, a lover of land. Without the seeds he planted in my mind, this book would neither have grown nor flowered.

PREFACE

Writing this book took only a year, but gathering and assimilating the knowledge necessary to write it took many years, and the help of many people.

This book was written because I found that the average buyer lacked a great deal of the basic knowledge necessary to make a sensible land purchase. This lack of knowledge was not the result of any inadequacy on the buyer's part; there are simply too many facts to learn and too many pitfalls for anyone uneducated in real estate practices.

In leading customers and clients through either land purchases or land evaluations, I found that they would quite often look at me with blank faces and perplexed expressions concerning points which were second nature to me. I had to keep backing up and explaining basic real estate points and legal facts in order to make a sale or explain an evaluation point. In doing so, I developed the system which finally, with the help of many people, evolved into this book.

In addition to Russel Uhland, without whose inspiration, help, and instruction, I would never have entered the land field, my thanks go my wife, Beverly, and my children, Laura and Mark, for putting up with the separations and frustrations of having a member of the family living in one place and working in several distant locations. And, additionally, I want to thank Beverly for her excellent guidance and comments in the preparation of this book.

My thanks also go to Mary Koach and Doris Kendrick for their invaluable help in proofing and preparing the manuscript; to Larry Anderson for his most excellent technical assistance; and to Hannah Reich, my editor, for her very diplomatic and gentle way of correcting my errors and nurturing this book through its final stages.

In the end, this book is a product of my experiences on and with land over the past eighteen years. During that time I was helped by a variety of people, many of whom had no idea how much help they were—people like John and Julia Bize, with whom I designed my first roadbed and who were with me at the beginning of my land career; Charles Cassell, who was immensely helpful to me in making the sometimes-difficult transition from dealing in the urban community to dealing in the rural community; Howard Brown, Troy Smith, and Frank Cox, who each in his own way helped me a great deal in coming to understand land and how it can work either for you or against you; and to Raymond Vanover, Richard Brewer, and Leroy Sloper for their friendship and invaluable help during the years that this book was evolving.

I sincerely hope this book will help prospective land buyers as much as these people have helped me.

L. John Wachtel
Winston-Salem, North Carolina

1

A BOOK FOR BEGINNERS

This book will teach you how to buy land sensibly, effectively, and efficiently. It will not tell you how to make a killing in the real estate business; nor will it teach you how to buy a condominium or buy or build a house. What it is designed to do is to give you a basic understanding of buying land, be it off some dirt road or in a planned development.

This book is written primarily for the novice land buyer who wants a step-by-step guide through the experience of finding, checking out, and purchasing a specific piece of land, whether in the mountains, on the plains, or by the ocean. In addition, this book provides a detailed glossary of words commonly used in land dealings, as well as a technical soil glossary, so when you come across unfamiliar words in books and contracts, you will know what they mean. It may be wise to go through the first glossary before you read this book, paying attention to the starred words. There are also samples of the different forms and documents which you may come across when you are purchasing land. These forms are depicted and described in detail.

Finally, there are specific checklists which you can use at various stages of your land investigation—checklists to help you decide whether a certain piece of property truly does meet your needs. All these aspects lead to one all-important goal, which is to help you answer the underlying basic question which you must answer before making the final decision as to where and what and how you will buy—the question of the suitability of the land to your needs.

(opposite) If the activities you like best are done in coastal areas, don't settle in the mountains. Snowcapped mountains and alpine tundra are great for people who love the winter.

2

WHAT IS REAL ESTATE?

By law, property is divided into two categories—real property and personal property. *Real* property is land and its attachments. Attachments can mean a house, a fence, a barn or shed—anything that is permanently attached to the land. Everything else you own is called *personal* property. Any of your other possessions, your cars, jewels, stocks, and bonds, even though they may be worth thousands more than the land, are still personal property, not real property.

Watch what you sign! In law, land is considered all-important, so the law specifies that a contract for buying or selling real estate must be in writing and signed by the parties charged. This simply means that when you're buying a piece of land, you can't just verbally agree to the sale; the contract has to be in writing, and must be signed by both buyer and seller. On just about every real estate licensing exam, there is usually a seemingly silly question concerning someone writing a contract for land with something like lipstick on some out-landish item, such as a piece of glass. The question has to do with whether that is a legal contract. The answer is yes. If it's in writing, no matter what it's written on or what it's written with, it can be a legal and binding contract.

When you're buying land, unless you're sure of what you're signing, don't sign anything, not even a receipt. A receipt can be a binding contract, and you may find yourself liable for the purchase of the entire piece of property. What and when to sign (or not to sign) are just two of the many points covered in this book.

(opposite) Real estate means land and its attachments. The house, fences, and shed are all attachments. The camping trailer and the items belonging to the people on the porch steps are personal property. Land that has life in it and on it usually indicates good soil conditions.

3

THE MORE YOU KNOW,

THE BETTER THE BUY YOU'LL MAKE

Although buying land can be a very exciting and exhilarating experience, the nervous anticipation of owning your own piece of this planet Earth can be almost overwhelming. Be very careful. That same emotional high you feel when you first look at that "perfect piece of land" can be as detrimental as beneficial. It can blind you from seeing all the facts you should look into before signing on the dotted line. The more knowledge you possess and the more aware you are of all the facts, the less likely you'll be to make any mistakes.

Translated from Latin, *caveat emptor* means "let the buyer beware." Buyers *and* sellers both need to be aware of the laws governing real estate. Either may be hurt through their own carelessness or lack of knowledge. Instead of "let the buyer beware," I prefer to think of *caveat emptor* as "let the buyer *be aware*." Let the buyer get as informed as possible about the purchase that he or she is about to make. If you know what you're doing when you buy something, if you know all the facts about the item you're buying, you're going to make a better purchase. You're going to pay a more realistic price, and you're going to get a good return out of your hard-earned money.

Land, after all, is one of the best investments you can make, so long as you buy it wisely and don't let some misinformed or overzealous salesperson sell you something that you neither want nor need. As with any other kind of land purchase, be it purely an investment, a home, a second home, a farm, or simply something you bought so that you can watch the sun go down at a certain angle over a particular lake, buying land sensibly has to be done with a great deal of care, and only after checking out an entire variety of items and facts to make certain that the piece of land you're considering is going to suit your needs.

There is one crucial fact you must fully understand before you buy: *When you buy land, you don't simply buy land. What you really buy is the use to which you're going to put that land.* You may buy land for monetary reasons (to make a profit), you may buy it for utilitarian reasons (to live on or farm), you may buy land for aesthetic reasons (to look at, walk on, and enjoy its beauty), or you may buy it for reasons known only to yourself. Whatever the reasons, be certain your land suits your needs; that's what's important.

4

THE P.L.A.N.E. PLAN

There are some basic reasons for buying land. No matter how well-located or otherwise desirable a piece of land may seem, always ask yourself these basic questions: Does it please me? Does it suit my needs? Can I accomplish what I wish by buying this property?

To assist you in answering these questions, I've included a simplified form of the basic procedure I use in analyzing tracts of land for my clients. It's a simple five-step process which will help you gauge the worth of a piece of property to your needs. The five steps become very plain, once you're guided through them. To help you remember them, I've formed them into the word *plane.*

Price

Location

Access

Natural features

Everything else

Almost every course in real estate will teach you that the three most important aspects of buying land are: 1. Location; 2. Location; and 3. Location. No, that's not a typographical error. It's simply most real estate teachers' opinion. Although location is certainly very important, I disagree with the immense emphasis placed on it. In my opinion, price is actually slightly more important. If a piece of property is outside your highest and most extended price range, it is useless to you, no matter how well it is located or how appealing it is. You probably have a definite price above which you can't go, but your location requirements may cover a broad area of several square miles, or at least a certain section of town.

Price: When determining the price you are willing to pay, you need to make that determination even before beginning your land search, and then you actually need to decide on two prices:

1. The highest price you want to pay (one you can be relatively comfortable paying), broken down into the highest down payment and the highest monthly or yearly payments.

2. The highest price you can afford to pay if you make all the necessary sacrifices, in the event that you find an exceptional piece of property. This needs to be your upper limit—the price beyond which you cannot and will not go. (Again, figure both the down payment and installment payments.)

Setting these two price ceilings is very important. It will remove a great deal of the "spur-of-the-moment" emotion, and possibly save you a lot of grief over a wrong decision. By having your basic buying plan set, you will be better equipped to contend with the variable price factors which you will probably be faced with. For example, in considering the purchase price, remember to consider the terms as well. In this time of high inflation, it may well serve you to pay a higher price if the terms include a very low down payment and a long payment period at a reasonable interest rate. Also consider any removal or use value. Does it have a government allotment; can it be rented; does it have any decent timber? Take all aspects into account before determining the final buying price. These various aspects are outlined in the next chapter.

Location: Since you can't move land, location is almost as important as price. It is a factor with two stages of consideration: (1) The general location of the property, and (2) the specific location of the property within that general area.

1. In selecting the general location of the property that you are going to buy, you must be sure to consider more than just the obvious reasons for buying. For example, if you are a hay fever sufferer, is this area going to aggravate or help that condition? How about asthma, or other health or medical problems? You must be sure to consider those, along with your age and other physical factors, before deciding on a general area. Consider the terrain and the weather conditions, as well as your personal needs. Consider the things that you like to do, and consider your economic situation now—and what it might be when you move to the property. Check the state or area for such things as taxes, cost of necessities, and employment potential. Weigh as many different aspects as possible before you consider making your general-area selection.

2. Once you have selected the general area, you must decide what particular area within that general area will suit you best. You may not be able to determine this until you have studied the general area and visited several different places within it. Somewhere along the line, however, you will need to limit your search to one or two or three small areas within which you will make your final selection.

Just as in the selection of the general area, your choice of specific areas should be guided by similar questions. Try to picture yourself doing whatever it is you plan to do with the property. Whatever your reason for buying, try to determine your situation in relation to the general situation in your selected area. Keep an open mind and consider all sensible options.

Access: Third on my list of most important elements is access. This includes not only access to and from the property, but also access into various parts of the property as well as to all the things you are going to want to get to. You will have to decide how far from or how close you want to be to big city advantages.

Access is sometimes confused with location. Don't make the mistake of the man who bought a place just five minutes from a large town, then came to find out that it was five minutes by helicopter. For the average Joe, it was twenty-five minutes by car around a mountain.

Access to or into the property can come in a variety of ways. You can have access off a street or a public road which is owned and maintained by the state, city, or county. This is the best access to have. In some states it is the required type of access into a development. Another kind of access is a right-of-way, which means that you have the right to use a driveway or a road across someone else's property. Be very careful that it is a legally drawn, written, and recorded right-of-way so you don't wind up having to take legal action. Even though some sort of access usually cannot be denied, a verbal right-of-way can be taken away at the whim of the person who granted it, so it is relatively risky. For this reason, verbal access is something you don't want.

Access into the property is just as important as access to the property. Consider the time, labor, and expense of getting to the point on your property that you want to use, and add that to the cost of the land. After considering all the facts, ask yourself, "Does the access suit my needs?"

Natural features: This is a very important factor which includes topography, plant life, animal life, soil conditions, and general usability. Topography is the lay of the land, how steep, how flat, how easily a road can be built on it, how well the property will drain, and how difficult it will be to build on. The plant life and trees not only tell you if the soil is healthy, but indicate how the land has been used in the past and how it might be used in the future.

Animal life also attests to the health of the land, and whether any poisons or fouling elements exist in the soil. Soil conditions are all-important for water and waste disposal, pond or lake potential, growing gardens and building supporting structures. They are also indicators of possible water or wind erosion and salt-intrusion problems.

Everything else means just that—all the other things which will be important to you as a future landowner. Check for such things as bad smells (near a paper mill), loud noises (a neighboring airfield), or ugly sights (a junkyard or rock quarry). What good things are there? Streams, ponds, nice views, nice timber? Is the land zoned, or is a land-use plan in effect? Are there any land restrictions? The list is almost endless, and is different with each person. Later in this book you will find a sample list to help you in making your own personal list (Chapter 11, p. 54).

Each part of the P.L.A.N.E. Plan will be dealt with in depth in the following chapters. For now, keep in mind that in buying land everything must directly connect to the suitability of the land to your needs. It is highly unlikely that you will ever find the perfect piece of land. If you know your needs and are honest about sticking to what you want, you will eventually find something close to what you are looking for. The best advice is: *do not rush*, unless you absolutely have to (and then be very careful). Be slow and deliberate. Don't let anyone (most of all, yourself) talk you into a situation you may later regret. An impatient buyer is the target of con men and hucksters. Be patient . . . Take your time. If you miss out on that property you "just have to have," don't cry about it. Something as good (or even better) may be just around the corner.

5

SETTING YOUR PRICE LIMITS

By setting your price limitations, you'll save both yourself and your broker or realtor a great deal of time, effort, and money, since you won't waste time looking at properties outside your price range. As already mentioned, there are two ceiling prices you should determine: one which you can easily afford, and one which is your upper limit.

Your starting point is to determine exactly what assets you have. Many people have no idea what they are worth or how much they actually have of value. The help of an accountant or an attorney can be invaluable and well worth the fee. Generally, assets are comprised of: 1. Cash on hand, 2. Easily convertible assets (stocks, bonds, jewelry, gold, silver, etc.), 3. General convertible assets (furniture, garage-sale items, cars, boats, and other personal property which can, with some time and effort, be converted to cash), and 4. Loan-value assets (items which you cannot or do not wish to sell, but can use as collateral in order to borrow money—items such as insurance policies, stocks, or bonds).

Once you know what assets you can call on, you need to divide them into two classes—those you can easily part with and which you plan to use to purchase the land, and those which you could reluctantly part with, possibly with some hardship, if you found an extraordinary piece of property which you felt for one reason or another you had to buy.

Lastly, determine what two monthly payment amounts you can afford after you have made the down payment. It is usually foolish to pay cash for property (unless you have some tax or accounting reasons to do so). If you pay all cash, you use up money which you could be using to make profitable investments; in an inflating economy such as we now live in, you would lose the advantage of paying for your property in ever-decreasing-value dollars. Even if you have to pay high interest rates, if the terms are right you should come out very well in the long run. Find out exactly what terms the seller does want, or what terms are available from lending institutions.

If a seller is willing to let you pay something down, and then pay the balance over several years (it's called owner financing), the seller probably won't want to take over 29 percent of the total price in the first year. This is

14

because there used to be a law that if the seller took 30 percent or more of the total price on an installment sale (one that takes a period of years to pay off), then the government required the seller pay taxes on the entire amount of income from that sale.

For example, if you sold a piece of property for $10,000 and took $3,000 down, the government would charge you taxes the first year on the entire $10,000 rather than only on the $3,000 you actually received. That law is no longer in effect, but people change slowly, so normally, a seller will want 20 to 29 percent down, plus the balance over so many years at a certain percentage. Always check the seller's terms against terms you can get from several banks or savings-and-loan institutions. Shop around.

In determining your possible monthly-payment ceilings, use the same thinking with which you established the two down-payment amounts—one which you can easily afford, and the second based on sacrificing in order to make the larger payments. Once you know your basic buying price(s), you will be able to work them into your final price formula:

base buying price + income from land = buying price

In order to determine your land income, you need to consider what the property can possibly bring in. In many cases, the government dictates exactly how much of a certain crop, such as tobacco, can be grown on a parcel of land. This is called an allotment, and it goes with the land when it is sold. You can sell this valuable asset to someone who will take care of everything connected with growing, harvesting, and selling the tobacco, and pay you a certain percentage. In some cases, the sale of the allotment can actually cover the mortgage payments on a piece of property.

Another source of income may come from crops growing on the land when you buy it. Apples, nuts, citrus fruit, dates, avocados, grapes, wild rice are some examples. Such crops will require work to be profitable, but you can usually contract with local farmers to do the work, while you get a percentage of the profits or a pre-set fee.

Consider the rental value of the property. Neighboring farmers could use it to raise livestock. If it is near a town or city, it could be used for sporting events or outings by clubs or civic and service organizations. In some cases you might have to donate the land for such non-profit purposes, but many times they can find a business to sponsor them and pay you a rental fee. If there is harvestable timber on it, that is another source of income, and thinning out timber actually helps the other trees on the property.

Another possible source of income is renting the fields to a farmer. Still another possible source of income is from mineral or water rights. Check around the area and see if this potential exists. Lastly, see if there are any houses you could rent, and/or buildings or barns to store hay or other commodities. They can all be rentable assets and could bring you in enough money to cover that mortgage payment, possibly even bringing you some profit. You need to consider all of the possibilities in figuring your buying price. Once you have established your four ceiling prices, do not waiver. Do not allow your emotions to sway you from sticking to your limits.

PRICE-DETERMINING CHECKLIST

	AFFORDABLE PRICE		UPPERMOST PRICE	
	Down Payment	Monthly Payment	Down Payment	Monthly Payment

	1,000 CHECKING ACC.	200 GENERAL INCOME	2,000 CHECKING ACC.	350 GENERAL INCOM
Available	4,000 SAVINGS+LOAN	100 WIFE'S INCOME	10,000 SAVINGS +LOAN	200 WIFE'S INCOME
Cash				
on		200 PART TIME JOB		750 SECOND JOB
Hand				
	Total 5,000	Total 500 00	Total 12,000	Total 1,300

	5,000 STOCKS		15,000 STOCKS	
	3,500 BONDS		10,000 BONDS	
	2,000 GOLD COINS		5,000 GOLD COINS	
Easily				
Convertible				
Assets				
	Total 10,500	Total _____	Total 30,000	Total _____

	2,000 SALE OF HOUSEHOLD ITEMS		4,000 SALE OF HOUSEHOLD ITEMS	
	20,000 SALE OF CITY LOT		20,000 SALE OF CITY LOT	
General				
Convertible		250 (YEAR) GARAGE SALE		250 (YEAR) GARAGE SALE
Assets				
	Total 22,000	Total 21 (MO)	Total 24,000	Total 21 (MO)

	5,000 INSURANCE POLICY VALUE		20,000 INSURANCE POLICY VALUE
Loan	10,000 MORT. REFINANCING		50,000 MORT. REFINANCING
Value	5,000 2ND MORTGAGE		10,000 2ND MORTGAGE
Assets			

Total 20,000   Total _____   Total 80,000   Total _____

	2,000 INITIAL TREE CUTTING	500 (YEAR) ALLOTMENT	2,000 INITIAL TREE CUTTING	500 (YEAR) ALLOTMENT
Potential		500 (YEAR) TREE CUTTING		1,000 (YEAR) TREE CUTTING
Land		500 (YEAR) GRAZING		500 (YEAR) GRAZING
Income				

Total 2,000   Total 125 (MONTH)   Total 2,000   Total 166 (MONTH)

GRAND TOTALS 59,500   646   148,000   1,487

During your preparation process, price will usually become intertwined with location. As you begin your search for that special piece of land, you will soon find that certain locations are well outside your budget, while others, although well within your budget, are just not what you want. You can't expect to find oceanfront land or lots in an exclusive subdivision selling for $500 per acre, or a mansion at an exclusive mountain resort selling for a price of a five-room duplex.

In buying land, you will usually find the basic law of buying and selling generally applies: You get what you pay for. If you want a piece of land which has not been improved, perhaps is somewhere off a back road in rural America, not too near any special town or city, not on a lake or by the ocean—just a nice five- or ten-acre place no one has spent any money developing—you can expect to buy it at a fairly reasonable price. But if you buy in a development, on the ocean, by a lake, next to a golf course or ski slope, or in the middle of Palm Springs, you will have to pay enough for the land to pay the developer for all his work, plus a profit. So, in determining your ceiling prices, keep location in mind, so that you pick a reasonable set of price ceilings.

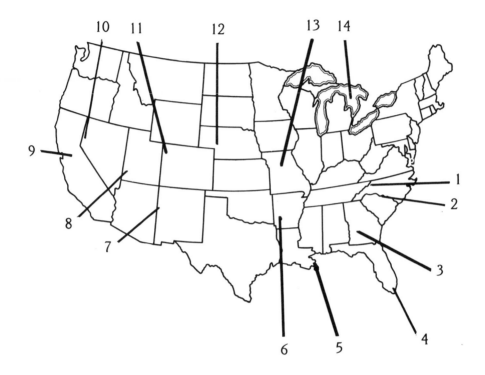

1–Appalachian Mountains	8–Great Basin
2–Piedmont Plateau	9–Coastal Range
3–Coastal Plains	10–Cascade and Sierra Nevada Mountains
4–Florida Tropics	11–Rocky Mountains
5–River Delta	12–Great Plains
6–Ozark Plateau	13–Central Plains
7–Desert Southwest	14–Great Lakes

6

PICKING A GENERAL LOCATION

You probably have a general idea where you want to buy land. If not, this is the next decision you must make. In making this decision, remember the basic question: Does it suit my needs and/or desires?

In selecting the general area, keep in mind such things as personal medical needs (don't opt for the mountains if you are a chronic hay-fever or arthritis sufferer). Not that being snowbound in the mountains isn't a delightful experience, but if you're a senior citizen and you have some health problems for which you might have to get to a hospital rather quickly, it is not the most sensible thing to do.

If you are buying property which you intend to do nothing with for the next 20 years and then retire to someday, try to picture the area as it will be at that time. Picture yourself fitting into that area at that time. If you're a sailing buff, don't pick a desert. If you like to snow-ski, don't select southern Florida, and if you're an avid water-skier, don't pick the northern climes unless you're willing to give up water-skiing for most of the year.

If you like exotic foods and a heavy nightlife, don't pick a small-town environment—you'll be bored. Conversely, if the quiet beauty of small-town living appeals to you, don't jump into the hustle and bustle of big-city life. Financial considerations are as important as the physical ones. Does the state have an income tax? Some states don't, so your cost of living might be less.

In short, analyze your life-style, or what you want your life-style to be, and pick a location which will best suit it. Too many persons don't stop to consider this factor until it is too late. The time to determine where you want to settle is not after you start searching, but *before* you even let your best friend know you're looking.

Begin by choosing a large general area, a section of the country, a state, or a group of states; then look at smaller places within that large area. Try to pick several areas, and know the reasons you are picking them. Remember, the smaller the areas you work with, the easier it will be to pinpoint the specific place in which you wish to buy. The larger the areas you start with, the longer the process will take. Unless you have unlimited funds, try to select an area of no more than 100 to 200 square miles in diameter. That way, you are approximately two hours by car to the farthest point from its center.

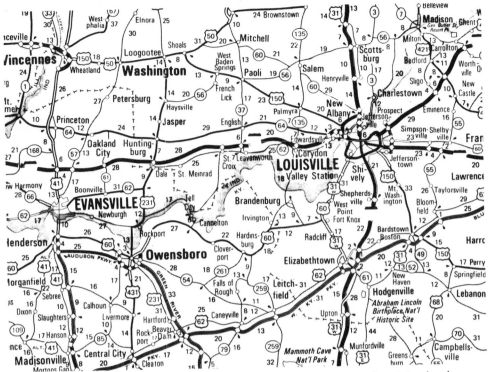

When selecting an area, make certain that there are centers of activity (such as towns and cities) near enough so that you can do the things you want to, and a good road network to reach those places. Acquiring a good county map can save you a lot of trouble in finding rural property, especially when you're trying to do so on your own.

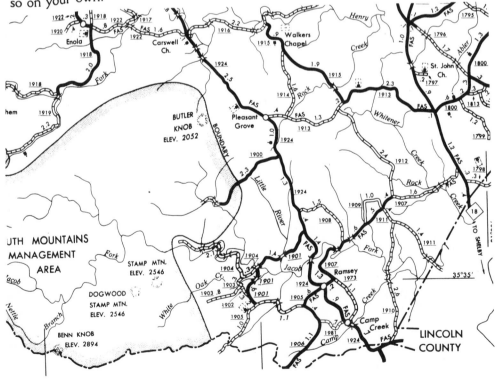

7

FINDING THE SPECIFIC LOCATION

Now that you've established your price ceilings and determined a general location, you are ready to begin the final process toward finding that particular piece of property which will suit your needs. Begin by listing the towns and cities within your selected area which have newspapers. In a large city, there are usually two or more daily newspapers and possibly several weekly papers. Try to get copies of each one. Armed with your list, go to your hometown library and ask the reference-desk librarian for a source book which will give you the names and addresses of the newspapers in the towns on your list. Write to them. Tell them you are interested in moving into their area. Ask them to send you several back issues of the papers. Ask for their subscription rates, and be sure to include a couple of dollars to cover handling. If they want more, they'll let you know. Ask them to send several entire papers, not just the real estate sections. The papers will give you a beginning feeling for each area.

While you're waiting for the papers to respond, contact any friends or relatives in your area of interest, or talk to some of your closer friends and find out if they know anyone in that area. Write to these people. Tell them why you're writing and what you're looking for. Ask them if they know of any land for sale, or of any real estate persons whom you might communicate with. Friends provide an excellent entrée, but remember when dealing with friends to be careful and still follow all the rules. Well-meaning friends are not infallible. Check with the real estate brokers in the area where you now live; they may know of land in the area in which you are interested. If you wish, you can hire a broker to help you search for your land. Some brokers will take on such a task at no cost to you (they share in the total commission paid by the seller), while others will require you to pay them a fee.

When you receive the newspapers, look through them in a general way. Consider that if you move into the area, you will become part of that community (in only a small way perhaps, but a part, nonetheless). Read the main stories to find out what is going on in the area. Look for names of prominent businessmen and community leaders; write down their names for later reference. Look through the store ads to see·what kind of merchandise is available in the area. Many small-town papers have "lists of services"; these will show you the extent of the service community (after all, you will need plumbers, electricians, etc.).

Finally, look through the real estate section and see what properties are for sale, and note the names and addresses of the real estate brokers. Make a list for later use. If any ads catch your eye, write about them and ask for complete details. Once all the papers you wrote for come in, try to put together all the information you have been able to glean on each town or area. Discuss these different areas with your family. Give each area the ultimate test: *Would this area suit my needs and desires?*

If you had selected the general area of Virginia, North Carolina, and South Carolina, then you have the option of a seashore, a piedmont (or a "foothills" area), and a mountainous area. You must now decide which of these three areas is going to best suit your needs and the life-style which you intend to follow. Another major consideration is just how close you want to be to a major city or town. Here again, if you have chronic health problems for which you may need specific care, you certainly want to be close to a good medical facility which is fully equipped to handle your particular needs.

You will probably never find exactly what you're looking for and will likely have to compromise to some extent. Imagine, for example, that you would like to have a farm within 20–30 miles from the city in which you are now living. You find one 25 miles away and one 50 miles away. Don't immediately discount the one farther away. If the one 50 miles away is less expensive, has better soil conditions, and the topography lends itself better to your needs, then certainly you might opt for it, rather than the closer one.

By the same token, if the soil on the closer farm is boggier, or if the closer farm is so close to the city limits that it may be annexed into the city and farming no longer be permitted on it, you may decide the 50-mile-distance farm's advantages outweigh the drawback of the extra 25 miles.

Try to narrow the field down to at least three, or possibly two, areas. If you can, it may be wise for you to take a quick drive through each town under study. This may be impossible, but do it if you can. After a careful analysis of all the facts, you must make that all-important decision to narrow down your search as much as possible. Guide yourself by time and your pocketbook. If your purchase is still years in the future, and you can afford the necessary time and money, then by all means check out all possibilities, and even some of the seeming non-possibilities. The process could take years and occupy all or much of your free time. If, however, you are among those of us who are limited in both time and money, limit your far-flung wanderings to television, travelogues, and your library's travel section. Then, after much armchair travel time is under your belt, sit down with all the available facts and select the specific area which will be your target. If you can't yet narrow it down to one, choose two or three areas to consider, but not more than that.

8

FINDING THE SPECIFIC

PIECE OF PROPERTY

Now that you've narrowed the field down to three areas or less, start your final elimination process. Get as much help as possible. You will find help at no charge from a variety of sources, including real estate brokers, land developers, and lending-institution officers. You can get their names and addresses from the local papers and from the local phone book, which you can purchase through the phone company where you now live, or by writing to the phone company in the area in which you wish to buy land. Write to each group of persons I've mentioned above. (Use *Sample Letter A* for real estate salespersons and land developers and *Sample Letter B* for all others.) Address each letter to the person in charge, if that name is known to you. If not, use the general salutation "If you please." This greeting will not be insulting to anyone, male or female.

Sample Letter A
IF YOU PLEASE:
Your area has interested me to the point where I would like to look into purchasing a tract of land within (*one half-hour's, one hour's, two hours'*) drive of (*town's name*). I can consider a price of up to (*85% of your easily affordable price*) or slightly higher if the property is truly exceptional. It would be nice if the property had (*a stream*) (*a pond or lake*) (*nice timber*) (*good pasture for grazing*) (*nice views*) (*an old restorable house*) (*ocean beachfront*) (*any other amenities you want*). In listing the properties you have to offer, please give me the following information about each: Asking price, number of acres, exact location in relation to (*the town*), what kind of access, topography (*what percent steep, what percent wooded*), any structures, its best present use, what amenities it has, what drawbacks it has, and whether you have the exclusive rights to sell.

Sincerely yours,
(your name and address)

Sample Letter B

IF YOU PLEASE:

I am writing to ask your assistance in locating a piece of property near your town. I have already written to several brokers, so I thought I would ask you if you know of any direct, distress, auction, or tax sales in the area within *(number of hours)* of your town.

I will appreciate any assistance you can give me in this matter.

Sincerely yours,

(your name and address)

Your letter to the real estate companies should bring several good responses; the other letter may get you a lead or two, but usually will not be too fruitful. What it *will* accomplish will be to pave the way for you later on when you are in town checking out a piece of property.

When the responses come in, go over them carefully and pick out the most interesting ones from each broker's office. If you responded to any ads, check to see if any of the responses concern the same tract—sometimes you will get contradictory information. Don't wait for all the brokers to respond, but write to each as they come in. After you have selected the one or two properties which interest you the most from each broker, send that broker the following questionnaire to fill out. Send one questionnaire for each property, and leave out any items which do not apply.

Dear ___(Broker)___

Would you please send me the following information about the _____
_HERMAN MORRIS_____ tract: TOTAL PRICE $50,000 TERMS:
% Down 25% Balance _14_% _3_ Years. TOTAL ACREAGE _27.5_.
LOCATION _IN (COUNTY) ON S.R. 421_____.
How long has property been for sale? _6 MO._ Distance by paved road ✓____
or gravel road is _3_ mi. to _(COUNTY SEAT)_____. Closest grocery store
____I MILE_____Gas station ____½ MILE_____Shopping
center __I MILE_____Restaurant __I MILE_____Hospi-
tal __5 MILES_____Fire Station __2 MILES_____House of
worship _3 MILES_____ Other _POLICE STATION   4 MILES_____

ACCESS: Surface of access road _PAVED___. Who maintains? _STATE___ If
publicly maintained, how much frontage? _300'___ If right-of-way, how wide?
_N/A___ Is it deeded? _N/A_ Is there a road onto the property? _YES___
What surface? _GRAVEL___How wide? _16'_____Who maintains?
_OWNER_____ Does anyone have easement over this road? _NO_____
(list party[ies] on back)

NATURAL FEATURES: Stream front _✓_, river front (view) _____,
lake front (view) _____, oceanfront (view) _____. Are there scenic views?
YES big trees? _✓_ dunes? _20_ % of steep land to flat _80_%. In
timber _50_%. In pasture _50_%.

AMENITIES: Is there a survey? _YES_ Do you have a plat? _YES_ Do you
have a topographic map? _YES_ Is power on or to the property? _YES_
Telephone? _NO_ Fences? _YES_ Ponds? _NO_ Sewer? _NO_

DRAWBACKS: Any noise? _NO_ pollution? _NO_ foul odors? _NO_
drainage problems? _NO_ Is this a distress or estate sale? _NO_

In your own words, please describe this property and tell me why it is a good
buy. _IT IS A NICE SMALL FARM AND WOODLAND TRACT —_
HAS SOME TIMBER VALUE AND A VERY PRETTY STREAM
RUNNING THROUGH IT. THE PRICE IS UNDER OTHER
COMPARABLE TRACTS DUE TO OWNERS NEED TO SELL
QUICKLY.

Please send picture(s) of the property, if possible.

Broker's name, address, and phone: _____

Do you have exclusive rights to sell this property? _YES_

There will be some brokers who will not fill in this form, but will call you
and try to get you to come see the property. Use your own judgment as to what
you do, but keep in mind that the broker who will take the time to fill out this
form will probably do a more complete job. It's a good way to weed out the bad
properties and the lazy brokers. Most brokers will be happy to fill out the
form, primarily because it saves them time in qualifying you as a potential
buyer. If you call them back after they have filled in that form, they know that
you are a serious buyer and they will treat you accordingly.

Once you have these forms back, you should be able to narrow the field
down to two or three good possibilities. Don't discard the others, simply put
them aside; you may go back to them if the properties you picked first don't
work out.

9

THE FIRST LOOK

(A general appraisal of access, natural features, and amenities)

Unless you are buying land purely for investment and know exactly whom you are dealing with and what you are doing, never buy any land without seeing it, and, preferably, walking or driving on it. Buying land sight unseen is the easiest way to get parted from your hard-earned money. No matter how good the deal seems to be, no matter how urgently the salesman tries to push you, don't be trapped into an emotional has-to-be-today buy; it can mean trouble. The only safe way to buy land is to follow a step-by-step investigative process, part of which should be to physically see or be on the property.

Before you leave to visit the first broker or owner, arm yourself with all the responses he or she sent you, both the ones that sounded very interesting and made you decide to make the trip in the first place, as well as any others you may have received. Sometimes one that doesn't sound so interesting on paper turns out to be better property after all. Take some blank forms in case you're shown different properties.

If you're dealing with a broker, try to make arrangements to meet at the broker's office. It will give you some insight as to the type of person that broker is, and possibly which associations or service organizations he or she belongs to. I don't mean to imply that all brokers need to have plush offices, but if the office is well-kept, orderly, and neat, then you can assume that the broker is a caring person and should do a fairly complete and careful job for you. However, if the place is messy, or if the broker or the employees seem to be running around in confusion, you will want to check to make certain that they're following through and doing their jobs properly. Detail work is a broker's stock and trade. If not done properly, it can wind up costing you time,

---

(opposite) Always consider the direction in which the town near your new property is developing. Urban growth is usually a positive factor, but not when it ruins your view or hurts the value of your land. Also, what you find along the access to your property is extremely important. Be sure you like what you see. Small-town living presents views you might enjoy seeing every day.

money, and heartache. If a broker won't meet with you at the office, send your antennae up and be very careful.

Once you've met the broker or owner and chatted a little about the area in general (remember that you may become part of the community in which you buy land), get some idea of what this community is like. Find out the direction the town is developing in. If you're looking for a secluded ten-acre place, you don't want to buy it on the side of town where industry is going to nibble at the edges of your Shangri-la. If you're buying in order to develop the property into lots, you want to make certain that the residential building flow is in the direction of the property you are buying. This is general-information time. If one of the pieces of land you will see really appeals to you, you can get more specific details later.

If you have contacted a typical broker, he or she will usually want to show you at least three pieces of land. Brokers often show you two pieces they don't think will be what you want, and then show you the piece they want to sell you. The first two usually won't compare to the third, so the result is supposed to be that you will be so impressed with the third that you will immediately buy. Make certain that you have allowed enough time to see more than three pieces. Get as much comparison as possible. Don't fall into the self-imposed trap of saying that your time is limited; take the necessary time so that you are not sorry later for making a hasty decision. If necessary, stay an extra day in the area. Your buying decision is too important to rush.

As you are driving to each property, take out the appropriate review sheet. If it's a new property, fill in one of the blank ones you brought with as much information as the broker can give you off the top of his or her head. Get as much information on that property into your head as possible. Finding the right piece of land is like trying to put together a giant jigsaw puzzle. The more you can remember as new facts come at you, the better the decision you will be able to make. Ask the broker or owner to tell you when you will be a mile or so from the property. At that point, begin to take more detailed notice of what is along the roadside; consider if you like what you see. Remember, if you buy this property you will possibly be driving this way, so will your friends, and possibly your customers.

If the property has frontage on the approach road, ask the broker to stop at the property corner so you can see how the line runs from that corner. If there is a plat or survey of the property, refer to it. Have the broker drive you to the other end of the road frontage so you can see all the land along the frontage access road. If there is a road onto the property, drive or walk on it.

Access (the "A" in P.L.A.N.E.) to and into the property is the third-most-important consideration, so begin a careful analysis. At this point, try to get a good general picture of the property, how it lies, which direction it stretches in, how it looks to you. From first appearances, will it suit your needs and desires? If all or some of the corners of the property can be seen from one spot, ask the broker to point them out. If not, and the parcel is small enough, walk to where you can see the corners, or walk to the corners themselves. Check the boundaries with the survey or plat (if there is one), or ask whether the purchase can

Beginning at a point on Rustle Lane East and running South 88–44–30 East 273 ft. to a branch; thence continuing with the meanders of said branch South 09–56 East 121.23 ft. to a point in said branch; thence leaving said branch and running North 88–44–30 West 301.00 ft. to a point on Rustle Lane East; thence running with said road North 09–52 East 54.64 ft. to another point; thence continuing North 02–00 West 65.00 ft. to the beginning and containing 0.776 acres more or less and to the center of Rustle Lane East along the frontage of said lot.

A typical rural survey description.

---

be made pursuant to a survey. Ask if the seller will pay for the survey. You may have to pay for it. If there is no survey, make certain that the sale is contingent on a survey before closing. Many rural tracts are sold "by the boundary," and described by very old "calls," using tree stumps or rocks as calls and corners. It's all very legal, but sometimes hard to follow. On such boundary surveys, the acreage figure is usually followed by the words "more or less." That legal "more or less" can mean a considerable difference in acreage from that noted on the map or plat, and you might be the loser. Don't take chances. Most surveys are rather costly, but insist on a survey, even if you have to pay for it. In the long run, it will usually be money well spent.

Once you have satisfied yourself that the ground lines correspond fairly well with the survey, start reading over the checklist the broker mailed back to you. Do all the visible items check? Go down the list point by point. If anything seems wrong, ask the broker for clarification. Take your time, look the property over carefully, ask all the questions you can think of. If the broker is staying too close to you and you want to discuss something privately with your spouse or companion, don't be embarrassed to ask the broker to let you speak privately. The broker will understand, and you won't be hurting his or her feelings.

Be sure to write down your thoughts and feelings on the back of the property sheet. You may see several properties before you see this sheet again; make sure you can identify the property in your mind from the notes. Most of all, and possibly most difficult of all, try to picture what you intend to do on or with the property once you buy it. If you are buying it as a home place, try to picture where the house would go and how you would put the driveway in. If your intention is to break up the parcel and resell it, consider how difficult the road-building would be, and whether there would be enough land to break up into desirable lots. Whatever your purpose, try to envisage your intentions on that piece of land.

Do the same with every piece of property which interests you. There will be some properties you'll tend to turn down the moment you see them. That's fine, as long as you don't jump too fast. Sometimes a property which seems to be totally unacceptable at first glance turns out to be just the thing upon closer examination. Allow at least an initial look at each property. If nothing else, this will give you something to fall back on if none of the others work out, or if the property you decide on is sold before you can get back to the broker.

Once you have visited several properties (with possibly more than one broker), try to catalog the properties in your mind and then make a selection order of interest. If one property is very high on your want list, and you feel that you may buy it, call that broker before you leave town. If you're still with the broker, explain that although you still have several tracts to see in another area, you're very interested in such and such a tract. Although the broker can't hold a tract for you without a deposit, it will inform the broker that you're interested. If the broker has a bid on the property below the asking price, he or she will advise the client that there is another interested party. You may thereby prevent losing the property when and if you come back to buy it.

Once you have visited all the various properties which you selected from the initial question sheets, you should be in a position to make a list of preferences. You should have one, two, or at the most, three properties which fit your needs and desires and which you want to buy.

10

THE IN-DEPTH INVESTIGATION

OF THE PROPERTY

Your in-depth investigation of the property should, if at all possible, be done on two visits. First, pick a bright and sunny day for your main visit so you can see the property at its best, and then come back during a downpour or on a day that's cloudy and overcast. That way you'll also see the property at its worst. The broker or owner will usually be delighted to give you a second look. If you go back alone, get permission to do so; it makes for better feelings all around. When you do go back, dress accordingly. Wear a good pair of walking or hiking shoes. (By the ocean, you'll want shoes you can put on and take off easily; also plenty of suntan lotion is in order.) Take a small jar (to bring back a soil sample), a small shovel, a bulb planter, a camera, compass, and checklist. Keep in mind that you're going to check *access, natural features, and everything else*, the last three items on the P.L.A.N.E. plan.

What you are looking for are the same things you would look for when you see a house, or anything else of value. When you examine a house, you can immediately tell if it's shabby, clean, well-kept, run-down, in need of paint, etc. You can tell the same about a piece of property. Look for piled-up junk, dead trees or other vegetation, stagnant water, marshes or bogs, foul odors, erosion of the soil, signs of wind or wave damage, rampant weed growth, such as water hyacinth or kudzu, absence of much vegetation, absence of animal signs, or just a general rough look. Be aware also of signs of excessive wheeled traffic.

None of these things necessarily means that a piece of land is bad or a poor buy. What they tell you is the condition of what you're buying. The price needs to reflect these conditions, and you should be forewarned as to what work or corrective measures you will have to take in order to put the land into the condition you want it. You'll naturally pay more for a piece of property which has no bad points or drawbacks than you will for a piece that will take some work and effort to make usable. At this point, let your common sense be your guide. If the month is July, in the northern hemisphere all leafy trees should be green. If they are brown or have a wilted look to them something is wrong. I realize that this example may seem a bit simplistic, but if you

31

approach every aspect of the property with the attitude depicted by that question, you won't go too far wrong.

Once you have a good general picture, start in on the specifics. Your first consideration has to be access into the part of the property you want to use. If a road or driveway exists, well and good; if there is none, then you will have to build one. The amount of effort and expense will depend on the type of soil conditions and obstacles. For example, if you're buying a 50- to 200-acre tract, and you want to put in perhaps as much as a quarter of a mile of road, you could be talking about a good deal of money. If the property is by the ocean, special care must be taken to make a good bed for the road while making certain that surface features, such as dunes, are not destroyed arbitrarily. Crushed seashells make excellent roadbeds.

If the property is heavily wooded, then you have to go through the considerably aggravating operation of cutting the trees, removing the stumps, grading the land (this involves bulldozers and other equipment), not to mention that you'll probably have to have someone lay the road out for you so that its grades are not too steep, it is sloped correctly, it washes properly, and is crowned enough in the center. This information can usually be gotten from a good dozer operator rather than having to go to an engineering firm. You must first ascertain that that dozer operator really knows what he is talking about. Ask him to show you some of the roads that he has constructed, so you can see what kind of job he is capable of doing.

Go over as much of the property as is practical; use a car, jeep, motorbike, boat, or horse, and, of course, your feet, but try to see the property all the way through. Look at the lay of the land, the topography. Are the flat areas boggy with standing water? Are the steep areas totally useless? Will the trees need a great deal of thinning out? Is there beach erosion? Does the way the land lies suit your needs and desires?

Next, look at the soil. The composition of the soil is important to you; it could be either sandy, rocky, composed of a great deal of clay, or what is called loam. The loam-type soil is what you find primarily in the woods and moun-

This is an example of good loam soil. It is mostly rich dirt with a moderate amount of rock through it. This type of soil usually percolates very well.

tains. It is a composite forest soil, a combination of clay and sand and small rock, together with vegetable and animal debris. When you walk through the forest, you will usually sink into the soft, loamy earth, made spongy by earthworms burrowing their way through it. At the seashore you will find a different composition of soil, primarily sandy, containing a good bit of rock, shells, and other residue of sea life, along with dead vegetation.

The easiest way to find out if the soil will meet your needs is to call the Soil Conservation Service and/or the Department of Health in the area where you are looking. Once you are seriously interested in a particular piece of land, make an appointment for them to come out and give you an initial soil opinion. Their free analysis of the soil will probably not include a percolation test (such tests are very time-consuming and costly), but the Health Inspector or SCS will usually be able to tell you whether the land is likely to perk, simply by knowing the soil conditions in that particular area.

Soil percolation indicates whether you will be able to use a septic tank system and whether the soil will be able to filter any impurities from whatever activity and structure you intend to put on it. Usually, you do not call the Health Inspector out until you have at least put an option on the property or decided that you are going to buy it.

Before you call in the experts, you can do some simple looking and testing for yourself. First of all, look at the land in general. Try to get as close to the middle of the property as possible, and look it over. Are there a lot of rock outcroppings? Are there bogs and tidal pools or other low, watery areas? Are there a lot of areas without vegetation? What is the color of the soil? Is it hard or spongy under your feet? If the land does have a lot of rock outcroppings, check it very carefully because it might be difficult to find enough deep percable soil for a septic-tank system. On the other hand, rock outcroppings, as long as they're not too prevalent, could mean shallower wells and fewer erosion problems.

Rock outcroppings on land can indicate percolation problems if the lot sizes are small.

If water stands in puddles such as this it may indicate percolation problems in the soil.

If you find standing puddles or small pools of water on the property, then you may have a problem with clay, and, again, soil that won't percolate properly. If there is very little or no vegetation in certain areas, it is necessary to check out why nothing is growing in the area, and find out what can be done to correct it. Sometimes the correction can cost you more than the entire piece of property.

Once you've given the tract a general inspection, pick out two places to core into the earth with your bulb planter. One place should be at a high point where the land goes down on both sides or on all sides, such as a ridge or peak; the other would be a low point, a hollow area. First, dig with your shovel. Dig an area about a foot across and a foot deep. Look at the sides of the hole. See how far down the surface moisture goes, or, if there isn't any moisture at the surface, how far down you have to go before you hit moisture. Take the earth and dirt in your hands—feel it—it should crumble as you work it with your fingers, but it shouldn't be too sandy (except in a desert or near the ocean where a high degree of sandiness is natural), and it shouldn't be of a clay consistency or mucky.

Next, take your coring device. Place it in the bottom of the hole, stomp on it, and get a good core sample as far down as you possibly can. Twist your corer as you pull it out so the dirt core stays inside the sleeve. When you get it out, turn it over and take out the bottommost particles of soil; work them between your fingers. The soil should feel and look just as it did at the top of the core. If it doesn't, have a soil analysis made.

When you are through with the coring and digging in the high area, move to a low area. Be sure you're not digging in a bog, stream, springhead, tidal area, or stream bed. In the lower areas of the property, you may have to dig a little deeper to get through the collected topsoil and surface moisture. Follow the same procedures as you did on the higher land. The soil in the low area may be a bit more moist than the higher area soil which was exposed to more of the elements and to better drainage; still, it shouldn't be boggy or extremely wet. When you are making your analysis of the soil, keep in mind the area of the country that you're digging in. If you are in the desert or by the seashore, then naturally the soil is going to be more dry than if you're digging up in the mountains or in a generally swampy area.

When you're done with your corings, don't throw the soil away; put some in the jar you brought and take it to the Agricultural Stabilization Control Service Office (ASCS). Give them the soil sample. They will analyze it at no charge, and tell you exactly what minerals and chemicals it contains. They will also recommend what the soil needs in order to be used for pasture, planting, or whatever use you intend for it. In some areas of the country, the government provides cooperative programs for fertilization of land which will be used for grazing.

Soil condition is one of the most important aspects of sensible land buying. Take the time to do a proper analysis. It may save you a great deal of grief. Next, examine the topography (the lay of the land). It can tell you a great deal. Land runs the gamut from depressed (which means it is so water-filled, so boggy, or so low that it has to be built up in order to be any good) to low, flat, rolling, hilly, mountainous, and, finally, alpine. If land is depressed, you need to find out exactly how much it is going to cost to make it usable. If it is low or flat, then you have to check to see that it drains properly, because if the rainwater falls on it and stands in puddles, it will eventually be a problem.

Rolling and hilly land is probably the safest land from the standpoint of proper draining and percolation. Here, however, you have to be careful of eroding soil, from washes after rains, and swelling streams which could cause flooding (much as they could with flat property). Lastly, with mountainous and alpine land, steepness is a great concern, although with the proper engineering you can easily build a house on the steep side of a hill.

Some mountain homes are built on land so steep that only the rear wall touches the ground.

In certain cases, houses are built on hills so steep that only the back wall of the house touches the ground, while the rest of it sits on pilings which are driven down to solid rock. An aspect of some higher-elevation land is the sparseness or lack of trees, and the scrubbiness of the foliage. This can lend itself to excessive drainage and erosion. Great care has to be taken when you are disturbing the soil—building a road or digging a foundation—so that it doesn't start excessive erosion.

One very good clue to good land is that it has life both in it and on it. Life, of course, takes the form of plant life (called *flora*), as well as animal life (called *fauna*). Examine the property for signs of animal life. Depending on the time of year, you should see some signs of living things. You may have to look rather closely, in the loam of the forest floor, on the sides of dunes, under rocks, in stream beds, on or in the trees, or at low tide. In some cases you may not be able to see the animals themselves, but you might find their burrows, their shells, their excrement, or some other traces they left behind.

If you find no signs of life, something may well be wrong with the property. Discuss this lack of life with the Health Inspector or the local Wildlife Officer of the State Forest Service. A healthy abundance of animal life is necessary for healthy soil. A forest would literally die if it were not for the earthworm churning up the forest floor soil, aerating it, and depositing its excrement as food for the plants and trees. You don't have to be an expert on animal or plant life to see the vital signs.

When building a road, even on flat meadowland, be certain to remove the top layer of sod. It will be damaging to leave it, since it will cause you problems later on, by not permitting the road to bond properly.

Cutting a road into a steep bank can be done rather easily. Just be sure to make it wide enough, to trim all the roots out of the bank and roadbed, and to slope and seed the banks whenever possible.

When entering a larger road or crossing a stream line, put in culvert pipes so that water can run under the road.

Look carefully at the land you're buying. A quick look at the vegetation growing on it tells you a great deal about how fertile the soil is. If the land has been used primarily for pasture, then check the grasses and the weeds that grow on it. Check the bushes that are springing up, especially in areas which grazing animals can't reach. You can tell good soil by the lushness, the green color of the vegetation (if it's supposed to be green, of course). Look at the trees and foliage. Do they look healthy? Are they the proper color for the terrain and season of the year?

Check the number of leaves on the branches of the bushes and trees, the fullness of the pines and the leafy trees, and the size of the vegetation in its immediate surroundings. If most of the pine trees, for example, are generally clumped together and sport thick green needles, or if the leafy trees abound with leaves, or if the grasses and clover and wild flowers have a fairly even admixture, then you know that the soil is fairly fertile and alive and well.

Check the insect and bird population. Look for birds and butterflies flying about. How many grasshoppers and crickets do you stir up as you walk through the grass? Dig about in some of the extra-moist loam and see how many worms you can find. All these are signs that the soil is good and alive. Their absence means to check further. Check for bare spots on the property. If you find some, try to find the cause. Is there an overabundance of some spreading plant, such as kudzu or water hyacinth? Either of these plants can envelop your property or pond or lake in a very few years if not controlled. Note anything and everything that doesn't look right to you, and discuss it with the Health Inspector or someone from the Soil Conservation Service (SCS) later on.

Look at the water conditions. If you're near the ocean, what is the extent of salt-water intrusion onto the property? Is fresh water available from wells? Is there beach erosion? This is now a major problem in coastal areas, and is a factor to check before you buy property by the sea. A good source of information about waterfront property is the United States Corps of Engineers, in addition to the SCS and ASCS. If you're looking at lowland, such as lakefront or river front property, check to see if it is in the hundred-year flood plain.

Water hyacinth is a pretty plant, but it can choke off ponds and streams if not controlled.

Uncontrolled weeds, such as kudzu, can completely take over an area.

Most of the land in America has been designated as to whether it flooded in the last one or two hundred years. If the land you are looking at doesn't fall in that category, it's unlikely to flood, although there's no absolute guarantee. If it is in the hundred-year flood plain, it certainly could flood again. Your SCS Inspector is the best source for this information.

If the property has streams on it, check for any signs of pollution (there could be a factory upstream, or a mine, or junkyard). If the stream looks clear, lean down close to the water and smell it. Make sure there is no foreign matter nearby, such as garbage or animal droppings. There should be no odor, except for a rich, forest "earth" smell. If you find a boggy area, dig down into it a bit. Try to find the source of the water. If you find a good flow of clean water, you could possibly have found a spring. If the flow is strong enough the year round, it could save you the cost of digging a well. Again, the SCS or Health Inspector can check it for you.

Make certain the land has been properly draining. This means that when rain hits it, it doesn't just stagnate in pools and ponds, but runs off. No land can support vegetation or crops or be used for grazing unless it is properly drained. Check the streams and springs. If you have a great many springs on the property, it may not be necessary for you to have a well dug if the springs can be capped off and kept absolutely clean. If you're going to need a well, don't assume that the lowest point on the property will be the best well site. It is impossible to tell exactly how deep a well will have to be to achieve enough water flow, no matter what the terrain is like. The best way to tell, primarily, is to go around the neighborhood and talk to the people who live there. Ask about the average depth of wells. Even then, well-drilling is so unpredictable that this method provides no guarantees. You can dig a well at one point and not hit water for 600 feet, then move no more than 10 to 20 feet, dig a well, and hit water at 100 feet.

The physical aspects of soil, topography, foliage, animal life, and water conditions are all *natural features* which go into the makeup of the land you're about to buy. If one or more of these aspects really doesn't fit into your plan, doesn't lend itself to the use that you want to put the land, pass up the property unless the bad aspect is fairly easy to correct.

Now comes the final part of the P.L.A.N.E. plan for buying land: *Everything else*. This includes the amenities, or favorable aspects of the land not mentioned elsewhere, as well as the detriments or drawbacks. Is there a beautiful view? Is there river frontage or ocean or lake frontage? Are there streams? Are there big trees? Is there timber on the property that could be sold now or possibly in the future? Is there an operating power line and/or phone line on or to the property?

Examine any structures and fences on the property. Are any buildings still usable? If not, is there any usable lumber in the old buildings? Check any dams or dikes carefully, and all retaining walls (if you're on the water). Then look for any drawbacks. What, if anything, is negative about the land? Are there any foul odors in the area? For example, is there a paper mill in the area? Is there a high level of noise? Is there an airport nearby? Is there some sort of noisy industry? Is there a motor-cross track or a racetrack nearby? Is there anything

Attachments such as derelict buildings can often be restored and made into valuable dwellings.

that would offend your sense of hearing or your sense of smell? Is there a garbage dump or a landfill in the area? Are there any legal detriments, possibly an estate sale? (This sometimes isn't told by brokers until you're well into the buy, but sometimes a piece of property is tied up with two, three, or four heirs, and when you make an offer, each of those heirs has to approve the offer, which means it can get to be quite a drawn-out affair.)

After you've found that there are no drawbacks which you can't live with, make an initial judgment and note it on the back of your analysis sheet. By the time you've seen two or three different properties, you should have some order of preference and several ways to tell the properties apart.

Drive around and talk to some of the neighbors. Ask such things as history of flooding, depth of average wells, and rate of the yearly taxes. Is the state or county pretty good about snow removal and road repair? Do any neighbors have any complaints about the area, or about other neighbors? Is there a high crime rate? Is there an airfield nearby? Are there any foul odors? How about fire protection and police protection? Is the rescue squad any good? Ask any and all other questions you can think of which would affect your enjoyment of your property.

Next, drive to the closest town. If it's not a county seat, you'll later also have to visit the county seat in order to meet with various persons whose offices are located there.

11

THE IN-DEPTH INVESTIGATION OF THE

AREA SURROUNDING THE PROPERTY

Now that you have checked out several parcels of land, go to the nearest town (preferably a county seat), and see if it will be the kind of place to which you wish to move.

CHAMBER OF COMMERCE

Your first stop should be the chamber of commerce. Here you'll usually get a warm welcome, along with a great deal of the information you'll need to properly check out the town. First, ask for a county map. Next, get any pamphlets or brochures containing information about the county, its government, services, growth forecasts, and its residential and industrial areas. Next, ask for a city or town map (there might be a slight charge). Ask someone to mark the location of the following: the phone company, the newspaper, the largest and smallest banks, the savings and loan association, the power and gas companies, the Health Department, the Building Inspector's office, the courthouse, the Soil Conservation Service office (SCS), the Office of the Agriculture Stabilization and Conservation Service (ASCS), the place of worship of your faith, a fraternal or service organization to which you belong, and a business (or businesses) similar to your own. You will need to stop at all or most of the above in order to get a complete picture of the town and the community into which you may be moving.

PHONE COMPANY

Your next stop should be to the phone company, especially if you did not get sufficient help at the chamber of commerce. While there, get a phone book (there is usually a charge) if you didn't acquire one earlier, and find out about phone installation. Using the county map as a guide, find out if phone lines extend out to the properties you are interested in. Ask about types of service available (private lines, party lines), rates, deposits, and if there is a waiting period for hook-up.

THE NEWSPAPER

Next go to the newspaper office. Speak with the editor or someone on the editorial staff about the general goings-on in the community which might affect your purchase. While there, pick up the two latest issues of the newspaper. Read them throughout the day, while waiting to see people, or at lunch. Compare them to any previous issues you have read, note any area changes and people in the news. See if there are any controversial issues which might affect any of the parcels of land in which you are interested. Mentally, compare the prices of merchandise with what you pay at home, and note if any clubs or organizations to which you belong are meeting during your visit. If so, attend the meeting.

THE BANK

Next, go to the largest bank; speak with the highest-ranking loan officer available. Tell the officer why you are there. Ask what percent the bank is charging for home loans and commercial (business) loans. Ask what percent of the total value of a house or of a tract of land the bank will loan. Find out in what part of town or in what area of the county most loans are being made (this will tell you if the land which you are looking at is in a desirable area). Be open with this person, especially if he or she is a responsible bank official. After all, if you are going to be active in this new area, a banker is a good person to have as a friend. When you have finished at the largest bank, go to the smallest bank and follow the same procedure. You may find some differences.

SAVINGS AND LOAN ASSOCIATION

Next, visit the largest savings and loan office. Speak with the chief loan officer (many small town savings and loans are branch offices in which the manager is the loan officer). Ask questions similar to those you asked at the bank. Savings and loan associations make more first-mortgage loans than do banks, so if you are considering building a house, this will be a very important person for you to know.

THE HEALTH DEPARTMENT

The person to see at the Health Department is the Health Inspector or Sanitation Engineer. This is a crucial stop, since this person is the one who will have to approve your lot or tract and sign your septic-system permit. The people at the Health Department are usually very helpful, as long as you remember their primary concern is the health of all the people in the district they serve, and not necessarily your particular desires. Check with these people *before* you decide on a site for your house. The location you pick may be the most beautiful part of your property, just by a stream, or with just the right view, but if the soil at that particular spot will not accept a septic system, you will not be permitted to build there without some expensive alteration to the ground, or possibly not at all.

It's vital that you discuss the location of the property with the Health Inspector before even considering buying the land. In many cases, bad, or poorly percable land will run in streaks or lie in specific areas. The Health Inspector will usually know what parts of his or her district have potentially poor soil. If the soil in the area in which you are interested is known to generally support septic systems, and you are buying a tract of more than two or three acres, you are fairly safe in assuming that somewhere on that property you will be able to put in a septic system. If the lot size is smaller, or if the area is known for poor percable conditions, it is best to ask the Health Inspector to come out to the land and analyze the soil for an opinion. Hopefully, he will find one or two places which will be acceptable. The services of the Health Department are paid for by taxes, so there will be no charge to you for the visit.

Another area in which the Health Department will be of assistance to you is if you find any springs or old wells on the property. If so, they can test the water to see if it is safe to use and drink. In order to check this water, one of the Health Inspectors will have to come out and take a sample directly from the source you are using. Don't bring in a sample; it will do no good. The sample has to be taken through a certain sterile procedure which only the Health Department people can do. What you need to do before a sample is taken is to cap off any springs or wellheads and run out some sort of pipe from which you intend to draw your water. Having done this, a sample can be taken. The Health Department can save you a great deal of trouble and problems, so be sure to meet with them early in your investigation and work with them as closely as possible.

BUILDING INSPECTOR

Next on your list is the Building Department Inspector. Even if you do not intend to build any structures right away, you need to check with this department to review their building codes in the event you intend to make any major improvements on your property. Such improvements include building a road, putting in a pond or dam, running electricity onto your property, or planning to sell some of your property off in lots. All of the above activities usually require a permit in most counties, and some counties totally prohibit some of the above activities. In the case of subdividing, some or all of the land you are buying for resale will usually be required to comply with a local or state subdivision code (or ordinance) which will dictate almost every aspect of the development process, from minimum lot sizes to turn radii of the roads. To prevent a great deal of wasted time and money, sit down with the Building Inspector and discuss your plans. Usually a few minutes' discussion will take care of a lot of potential problems.

AGRICULTURE STABILIZATION AND CONSERVATION SERVICE

This federal office primarily provides a farm service, but whether or not you intend to farm, raise a few head of cattle, keep some other farm animals, or simply keep fields in pasture, the ASCS people will be most helpful to you, both in giving advice and in possibly providing you with government co-op funds for such things as planting trees and spreading fertilizer.

That jar of soil you filled while inspecting the property should be brought to this office and left for analysis. After a week or so, you will receive a written analysis containing a great deal of technical information you likely won't fully understand. It will also contain instructions as to what to do, where to go to do it, and how much of it will be paid for by Uncle Sam. This office is not going to give you any free rides. The services and cooperative funding they offer are part of the farm assistance program, which is available to any landowner who meets specific criteria. Most of what you do on your land will have to be paid for by you, but the ASCS does have certain programs available for the asking. You might as well take advantage of them. After all, you pay for them through your taxes. The ASCS office will probably have an aerial photo of the property you are interested in. They can't give you an actual photo, but some offices have copy machines which can usually make you an adequate copy. They can also give you a fairly complete agricultural history of the property, including activities the current or previous owners had on the land, when the last crop fertilization was, and any other pertinent information the office may have on hand about the property. The ASCS office is sometimes in the same building as the Health Department and the SCS Office.

SOIL CONSERVATION SERVICE

Unlike the Health and Building Departments and the ASCS Office which have in-office staff personnel (so you can go there any time during normal working hours), the smaller SCS Field Offices usually do not have full-time in-office personnel. The best time to catch them is in the early morning, late in the afternoon (7:00–8:30 A.M. and 4:00–4:30 P.M.), on rainy days, or, best of all, by appointment. Most SCS personnel are in the field most of the time.

If you aren't lucky enough to catch them in, you might leave a note on their door, or plan to stop by at a later time. When you do get together, check with them about the hundred-year flood plain and any erosion problems they are aware of on this or adjoining properties. Ask if the land you are considering has the potential for a possible pond or lake site, and discuss your future plans

This soil map may not be very easy for you to understand, but it would be easily understood by a geologist or someone from the Soil Conservation Service. When you show them such maps, be certain that you have a copy of the code with you (it will appear somewhere in the soil book), in case local codes are used. (From the Virginia Division of Mineral Resources.)

in as much detail as possible. You'll find almost all SCS personnel very knowledgeable regarding land use, and usually very eager to help.

For example, if you want to put in a pond or a lake (which would mean damming a stream in the area), you need to find out from the SCS people whether a lake or pond is practical on this particular piece of land. They will come out, take a look at it, and advise you completely about building a pond, how to do it, what kind of dam you are going to need, and whether or not the pond or lake is likely to hold water.

The SCS people are also the ones with whom you will have to file a soil-erosion plan in the event that you are going to build a major road through the property or otherwise disturb a lot of topsoil. When the topsoil is disturbed, the undersoil becomes exposed to the weathering elements. This exposure can cause erosion on the property and possibly damage land downhill or downstream from this particular property. By law, the erosion of such excavations has to be carefully controlled, so be sure to check with the SCS people before you start any major land excavations on a piece of property. It is their job to help you and to protect both you and other landowners in their district in all matters having to do with soil and erosion.

THE COURTHOUSE

Your next stop should be at the county courthouse to meet with the tax collector (treasurer), the county manager (in larger counties one of his or her assistants), and the register of deeds.

In meeting with the tax people, ask what the present taxes are on the property which you are interested in and what they'll go to if you build or subdivide, or do whatever it is you intend. The tax collector may have to send you over to the tax assessor's office, but don't go there first; you may be able to get all your questions answered at the first tax office. The meeting with the county manager or agent should be about the plans for future growth in the county, i.e., what is going to happen in the next ten to twenty years, which areas of the county will be most affected and in what way. What you will learn will be a good barometer as to whether you want to live in this area, and just what aspect of this area's future growth (or lack of it) will best suit your needs.

A visit to the register of deeds will let you know the history (the abstract) of the property you are buying. (You will have to know the name of the current or previous owner.) This visit is not absolutely necessary since your attorney will make it later while he or she is performing the title search, but since you'll be able to see for yourself whether or not the land has any liens against it, or if the current owner doesn't have clear title, it may be worth it just for curiosity's sake.

THE ELECTRIC AND/OR GAS COMPANY

Utilities will be very important to you, so be sure to get the complete details about having electric and gas service at your property. If a power line has already been run to your property, you have a big factor in your favor. Utilities will almost always charge you for some phase of the hook-up unless it is to a permanent home a short distance (usually within 100 feet) of an existing power pole.

Different power companies operate differently in various parts of the country, so it is impossible to predict what kind of charges you will be facing. Sit down with that person at the power company who is in charge of the kind of service you are going to need. If you're going to need a line extension of, say 1,000 feet up a mountain, don't settle for talking to the fellow in charge of in-town service hook-ups. Make sure you speak with the line-extension supervisor. Remember, you're going to be dealing with a monopoly, so although employees almost always try to be polite and answer your questions to the best of their ability, they are under so many government controls and restrictions that it's impossible for each of them to know all the policies which may affect your service needs.

Each department is, however, very knowledgeable about its particular area, so if you're sure you're talking to the right person, you should be able to get some pretty straight answers. Once you have the necessary information, try to get a written confirmation for your records. When it comes down to exact charges, make certain everything is spelled out in writing, and that nothing is left in "verbal agreement." Many times the people who write up the deal don't do the work (sometimes the work isn't even done by the power company but by a private contractor), and the people who do the work will do only and exactly what is written down to do.

Treat the gas company the same way, although it is less likely that you'll run into as many problems since the gas lines will either already be extended, or simply not available.

THE PLACE OF WORSHIP OF YOUR FAITH

Your place of worship is an excellent place to get some relatively unbiased answers to any questions which were not answered to your satisfaction elsewhere. It's also the best place to discover the size and extent of your religious group in the area. Here, you might very possibly get some leads on some comparable land for sale, and/or contacts with a variety of persons who can be helpful to you in the process of finding, buying, and using the land you buy. Possibly getting some preferential treatment due to an introduction through your place of worship can smooth many rough spots in your road to owning that great piece of land.

YOUR SOCIAL OR CIVIC ORGANIZATION

This is yet another area through which you can get help with your quest. The quickly established rapport simply by virtue of your membership can often lead to some inside information, which may either speed you along in the buying process, or help you sidestep some not-so-evident pitfalls.

A BUSINESS SIMILAR TO YOURS

Here again, you can establish some fairly solid footing with someone who speaks the same business language as you do. You naturally have to consider that if you intend to stay in the same business and become competitive with this local person, then you may not get too far. But if you're retiring or if your moving into the area will not be detrimental to the local businessperson, then you should be able to expect some form of friendly assistance.

MAKING THE DECISION

When you complete all these visits you should have almost all the facts you need on each of the two or three properties you are interested in. You have studied all the plus and minus factors; you have discussed your findings with your immediate family. Now, ask yourself: Which of these properties best suits my needs and desires? Use the following step-by-step process sheet to write down all your findings, and then make that all-important decision.

IN-DEPTH ANALYSIS CHECKLIST

The following property evaluation survey is an all-encompassing questionnaire which you may have to change in order to fit your particular needs. Add to it or skip over things as you see fit. It is presented for you strictly as a guide. Any questions you cannot answer, ask of appropriate experts.

At the end of each stage of the investigation, you will find a 1 through 10 number evaluation system for your convenience. Where averaging is necessary (as it is at the end of the *Access* part), simply add up the three totals together and divide by 3. At the end of the *Natural Features* section, you divide by 5. Finally, after you have finished all the sections, place each of your section totals in their proper place on the front cover sheet, add them up and divide them by 5. This will give you a number rating for that particular piece of property which you can compare with other properties. This questionnaire follows the P.L.A.N.E. plan format, and begins with a cover sheet.

THE SUMMARY SHEET

This is a summary sheet which should be filled out as follows:

Property Checklist and Location—before you begin the investigation.

Access to property, Natural features, and Everything else—as you conclude each applicable part of the investigation.

Evaluation Summary—after you have completed your investigation and averaged the totals in each part.

Conclusions—after everything is complete and you can put your overall impressions into a very brief statement.

COVER SHEET

PROPERTY CHECKLIST—
   IN-DEPTH ANALYSIS
   Date ___4/16___

   Name and address of Owner/Broker
   _____
   _____
   Size of property __27.5__ acres
   Price $__50,000 °°__

EVALUATION
   SUMMARY
   P __8__
   L __9__
   A __8.7__
   N __8.8__
   E __9__
PROPERTY AVERAGE __8.7__

LOCATION:
   State _____ Nearest city _____ Nearest town _____
ACCESS TO PROPERTY:
   _____VERY GOOD_____

   Into property ___GOOD___
NATURAL FEATURES:
   _____BEAUTIFUL FLORA, AMPLE FAUNA_____
   _____

EVERYTHING ELSE:

Amenities _____ *NICE VIEWS, STREAM* _____

Drawbacks _____ *NO MAJOR, SOME MINOR EROSION* _____

General description _____ *JUST WHAT WE'VE BEEN LOOKING FOR* _____

Owner's reason for selling _____ *NEEDS CASH* _____

Conclusions _____ *WILL MAKE LOW OFFER, BUT COME UP IF OFFER IS REFUSED, SINCE PRICE IS LOW TO START WITH — WILL PAY FULL PRICE IF NECESSARY —*

PROPERTY CHECKLIST—IN-DEPTH ANALYSIS

GENERAL

Date of first visit _____ *4/15* _____ Weather conditions _____ *CLOUDY* _____

Date of in-depth investigation _____ *4/16* _____ Weather conditions *SUNNY*

PRICE

Asking price $ *50,000* _____ Within basic acceptable price ☑

Within uppermost acceptable price ☐

Terms: Down Payment $ *10,000* Balance _____ *3* _____ years at _____ *14* _____ %

payable to ☑ Owner ☐ Bank ☐ Savings and Loan ☐ Other (specify) _____

Release provisions *1/4 AT CLOSING AND 1/4 EACH YEAR*

Maximum term option available _____ *NONE* _____

Is second mortgage money available? _____ *NO* _____ If yes, from whom? _____

At what %? _____

Estimated closing costs $ _____ *500 00* _____

Possible income-producing features:

Saleable allotments _____ *NONE* _____

Pasture ____ ✓ ____ For grazing ____ ✓ ____ For cut hay ____ ✓ ____ Fishing Rights

_____ Hunting Rights ____ ✓ ____ Rentable dwellings _____ Other renta-

ble buildings ____ ✓ ____ Business rental _____ Water rights _____

Riparian rights _____ Oil or gas rights _____ Mineral rights _____

Potential sale of easement _____ Potential sale as lot development

____ ✓ ____ Potential recreational rental ____ ✓ ____

Comparable price evaluation:

Average price per acre of similar property, according to:

Big bank banker $ _1950 °°_ Small bank banker $_2000°°_ Savings and Loan executive $_2000 °°_ Broker/Salesman No. 1 $_1850-_ _2050_ Broker/Salesman No. 2 $ _2100°°_ Broker/Salesman No. 3 $_2000 °°_

If price of property is much lower, why? _____ OWNER NEEDS CASH _____

_____

Are there major drawbacks or deterrents? ___ NO _____

_____

If price of property is much higher, why? _____

_____

Are there major advantages and/or amenities? _____

_____

Final summary and comments on price: _SOMEWHAT LOWER_ _THAN COMPARABLE ACREAGE — PERHAPS I WILL_ _MAKE A LOW LOW OFFER AND SEE WHAT HAPPENS,_ _SAY $40,000 TOTAL — $8,000 DOWN WITH BAL OVER 5 YRS AT 12%_

Rate this property as to price on a scale of 1 to 10 and note the same number on Cover Sheet:

P—1   2   3   4   5   6   7   (8)   9   10

Conclusions and comments: _____
JUST THE KIND OF PIECE I'VE BEEN LOOKING FOR —
MINOR PROBLEM AREAS WITH EROSION, BUT
CORRECTABLE — HAS NICE VIEWS FROM POSSIBLE
HOUSE SITE.

LOCATION

State _NAME OF (STATE)_ County (Parish) _(NAME OF COUNTY)_ distance

from _(NAME) CITY OR TOWN   IN   3 MILES_ city or town
Is nearest town the county seat? ____ YES _____
Surrounding terrain: Mountains _____ Piedmont _____ Rolling _✓_
River(s) _____ Lake(s) _____ Ocean _____ Flat _____ Desert _____
Tundra _____

Climate: Average rainfall ___6 0"___ Average snowfall ___10"___
Average sunny days ___70 %___ Average temperature—Winter ___30°___
Spring ___70°___ Summer ___85°___ Fall ___70°___
Medical considerations: Mobility Potential ___GOOD___
Topography _____"_____
Weather conditions _____" , WITH EXCEPTIONS___
Special vehicle requirements _____NONE_____
Allergy potential _____GOOD_____
Activities potential: Business _____
Recreational _____EXCELLENT_____
Religious ___GOOD___ Family ___NOT TOO FAR___
Area plusses ___NOT TOO CLOSE TO URBAN AREAS___

Area minuses ___GOOD SHOPPING, SERVICES +
___RECREATIONAL POTENTIAL___

Rate the location of this property on a scale of 1 to 10 and note the same number on the Cover Sheet:
L—1   2   3   4   5   6   7   8   (9)   10
Conclusions and comments: _____
_____
_____
_____
_____

ACCESS

ACCESS TO THE PROPERTY
Off state, county, or city road ___SR 421___
Road surface: Macadam paved (hard surface) ___✓___
Concrete paved _____ Gravel _____ Dirt _____ Sand _____ Shell
_____
Is steepness of road a factor? ___NO___ In winter? ___NO___
Average width of road ___30'___
General description of roadside: Buildings, houses, any eyesores or drawbacks ___ONE JUNKY BUSINESS 3 MILES FROM LAND
___OTHERWISE NICELY KEPT BUSINESSES AND HOMES___

Through right-of-way: *NONE*

Width of right-of-way _____; Is right-of-way deeded? _____

If not, who has given undeeded right-of-way? _____

Is deeded right-of-way available? _____

Is an alternate deeded right-of-way available? _____

ACCESS INTO AND THROUGH THE PROPERTY

Does a road now exist on the property? ____*YES*_____

Description ___*GRAVEL JEEP ROAD - CAN BE IMPROVED AND USED FOR ACCESS TO HOUSE SITE*___

If no road, does a foot trail exist on the property? _____ Is there a good entry point off the public access road or at the right-of-way point? _____ If not, then an alternate right-of-way, if any? _____ Generally, it will be easy ___*✓*___ somewhat difficult _____ hard _____ very hard _____ extremely hard and costly _____ to build a driveway or road onto the property.

ACCESS TOPOGRAPHY

Does the lay of the land enhance ___*✓*___ or hinder _____ the building of a road?

Timber: Will timber removal be necessary for the building of a road? *YES* Can the timber be sold for lumber _____ pulpwood _____ firewood ___*✓*___?

ACCESS SOIL CONDITIONS

The soil conditions are rocky _____ sandy _____ mucky _____*LOAMY ✓*

Will these conditions enhance ___*✓*___ or hinder _____ the building of a road or a driveway?

POTENTIAL ROAD COSTS

Road layout $*NONE* (from local engineer or dozer operator). Tree, brush, and stump clearing $_*TRADE FOR PULP*_ Culvert pipes $*350⁰⁰* Blasting (if necessary) $__*—*__ Dozer $*600⁰⁰* Backhoe $*250⁰⁰* Gravel $*750⁰⁰*

ACCESS AND DISTANCE FROM THE PROPERTY TO AREAS OF INTEREST

Nearest: Town	*PAVED*	*3*
	(type road)	(miles)
Police *P* / *4*	Fire *P*	/ *2*
Ambulance *P* / *2*	Fast food store *P*	/ *½*
Bus stop *P* / *3*	Gas station *P*	/ *½*
Grocery store *P* / *1*	Local shopping center *P*	/ *1*
Major shopping complex *P* / *10*	Theater *P*	/ *3*
Fast food restaurant *P* / *2*	Family restaurant *P*	/ *1*

Fancy restaurant ___P___ / _3_ Doctor ___P___ / _3_
Dentist ___P___ / _3_ Place of worship ___P___ / _3_
School ___P___ / _2_ Drug store ___P___ / _1_

Recreation areas (fill in any appropriate, such as Beach, State and National Parks, Snow Skiing, Fishing, etc.)

___LAKE___ _P_ / _5_   ___FISHING___ _P_ / _5_
_____ / _____   _____ / _____
_____ / _____   _____ / _____
_____ / _____   _____ / _____
_____ / _____   _____ / _____
_____ / _____   _____ / _____
_____ / _____   _____ / _____
_____ / _____   _____ / _____
_____ / _____   _____ / _____
_____ / _____   _____ / _____

Rate each of the following three access considerations on a scale of 1-10, and note your conclusions concerning access:

Access to the property: 1 2 3 4 5 6 7 8 ⑨ 10
Access into the property: 1 2 3 4 5 6 ⑦ 8 9 10
Access to areas of interest: 1 2 3 4 5 6 7 8 9 ⑩

A—Average of Access ratings __8.7__ (Note on Cover Sheet)

Conclusions and comments: _____
___NO SPECIAL ACCESS PROBLEMS___
_____
_____
_____
_____

NATURAL FEATURES

Size of land __27.5__ acres. Shape of parcel ⬜ SORT OF SHOE SHAPED

Is there a survey? __YES__ Age of survey __4 YEARS__
Is survey certified? __YES__
General dimensions: Frontage __300'__ Width __300'-400'__ Depth __852'__
Is a topographic overlay or map available? __YES__
Is the land generally very steep _____ steep __✓__ moderately steep
_____ rolling __✓__ flat _____ depressed _____ reclaimable at moderate

cost _____ reclaimable at high cost _____ What % steep to flat? _20_ %
(steep). If treed, what % open _50_% (open). If there are evergreens, what %
to leafy trees? _80_% (evergreens). Is there a large amount of brush on the
property? _NO_ Is it flowering brush? _YES_ Does it enhance the property?
YES Is there vine type vegetation? _NO_ Is it a potential hazard? _NO_
Are there any income-producing crops? _YES_ ☐ Apples ☐ Citrus fruits
☐ Nuts ☐ Avocados ☐ Berries ☐ Pears ☐ Syrup ☑ Other _FEED GRASSES_
Are there plentiful signs of animal, bird, and insect life? _YES_ If not,
explain: _____
_____
_____

If there are pastures, do they appear to be in good condition? _?_ If not,
explain: _SOME SPARSE GROWTH, MAY NEED CORRECTIVE_
_____MEASURES_
_____

Are the soil conditions very rocky _____ moderately rocky _✓_ loamy
_____ sandy _____ clay _____ Is the soil very dry _____ moderately dry
_____ moderately wet _____ very wet _____ Will the soil percolate at the
proposed building site? _PROBABLY_ Is there any open erosion? _NO_ If yes, is
the erosion repairable? _____
Condition of dikes, dunes and/or sea walls, (if any) _NONE_
_____
_____

Are there any ponds or streams? _____ Are they clean _✓_ polluted _____
Average depth of wells in area _250'_ Is property in the hundred-year flood
plain? _NO_

Rate each aspect on a scale of 1-10, and note your conclusions concerning
natural features:

Topography	1 2 3 4 5 6 ⑦ 8 9 10
Soil Conditions	1 2 3 4 5 6 7 ⑧ 9 10
Trees and Foliage	1 2 3 4 5 6 7 8 9 ⑩
Animal Life	1 2 3 4 5 6 7 8 9 ⑩
Water Condition	1 2 3 4 5 6 7 8 ⑨ 10

N—Average Natural Features _8.8_ (Note on Cover Sheet)
Conclusions and comments: _____
SEEMS TO BE GOOD POTENTIAL TO GRAZE A
COUPLE OF CATTLE AND TO DO SOME MINIMAL
FARMING - WATER SEEMS TO BE IN EXCELLENT
SUPPLY
_____

EVERYTHING ELSE

Amenities (good things):

Are there any: Stream(s) ___✓___ View(s) ___✓___ Spring(s) _____ Dunes _____ Fences ___✓___ House(s) _____ Barn(s) _____ Shed(s) _____ Outbuilding(s) _____ Other _____

Is the property: Lakefront _____ River front _____ Oceanfront _____ How far from any of the above ___5 MILES TO LAKE___

Are the following available at the property? Power ___✓___ Phone _____ Natural gas _____ Water ___✓___

Drawbacks (bad things):

Are there any existing rights-of-way? ___NO_____

Are there building or development restrictions? _NORMAL COUNTY_ _ORDINANCES_____

_____

_____

Are there any: Foul odors _NO___ Excessive noise _NO___ Unsightly areas _NO___ Air pollution _NO___ Water pollution _NO___

Is the property near any: Paper mills _NO___ Junkyards _NO___ Chemical plants _NO___ Atomic reactors _NO___ Munitions plants _NO___ Heavy industry _NO___

Zoning or land-use plan ___NONE_____

_____

Taxes: Assessed value $_38,000ᵒᵒ_ Last year's property taxes $_380 ᵒᵒ_ Any special assessments $_NONE___

Weigh all the amenities and drawbacks, then rate this property as to Everything Else: E—1 2 3 4 5 6 7 8 ⑨ 10 (Note on Cover Sheet)

Conclusions and comments: _____ ___JUST WHAT WE'VE BEEN LOOKING FOR._____

_____

_____

12

BUYING THE PROPERTY

Now that you have decided on the area, found the specific piece of property you like, done all the checking, both of the property and the surrounding area, the nearest town, the county seat, and decided that this particular piece of land truly does meet your needs and is going to make you happy, you are ready to buy the land.

Now that you're ready, where do you begin? The proper place to begin is by making an offer, a very, very, low offer. It's usually at this point in the buying process that a buyer winds up paying too much for the land that he or she is buying by simply accepting the seller's asking price. The key at this point is to remember that the seller's asking price is rarely the bottom price, rarely the price at which he or she will eventually sell the property. The problem is that many buyers feel that it's undignified or insulting to counter-offer with a lower price. Because of this stuffy attitude, they wind up paying a good deal more for property they could have gotten cheaper had they made a counter-offer. The thing to remember is that this interaction between buyer and seller is a real estate transaction. A real estate transaction is a business deal, and in a business deal involving a buyer and a seller, the seller is trying to get the highest possible price for the property, while the buyer is trying to buy it for the lowest possible price. The process through which that final price is arrived at is called bargaining, and the bargaining process can't begin unless an offer is made. As an intelligent buyer, what you should do is analyze the price that has been placed on the land (check Chapter 11) and make a very low offer.

It is very difficult to tell just how much below the asking price to offer. Each situation is different. I've made counter-offers as low as 50 percent below the asking price, and then bought that property at 60 percent of the asking price. The seller dropped his price 40 percent. Only he knew why, but if I hadn't come in with a very low offer, I would have paid too much. The amount to offer depends on the particular situation, but, basically, you can use the general market as a guide. Remember, back in the checking-out process, you asked around to see what similar land was selling for. Review your notes and use them as a guide. You can be sure that if land of the type you're buying is selling for $1,000 an acre on the average, and it's in about the same condition as the type you're buying, then the seller more than likely knows that and isn't likely to sell it much below that price.

On the other hand, you don't know the seller's situation. The seller may need to sell, or may have purchased the land at a very attractive price and be willing to sell it considerably "under" market value in order to move it faster. These are all facts that you don't know, and the only way that you'll ever find out is by starting off with a very low offer.

All things being equal, I will usually make an initial offer on a piece of property somewhere between 5 percent and 25 percent below the market price. For example, on a piece of property which has an asking price of $50,000, I would not hesitate to offer $36,000 or $37,000. I don't make the offer expecting to buy it at that price; I make it in order to see how the seller is going to react. If the reaction is an immediate rejection, possibly with indignation and anger, then I know that the seller is going to be pretty hard to move and is going to be selling pretty close to his asking price.

On the other hand, if there is thought given to my proposal and then a refusal, or a counter on his or her part, then I know that there is a great deal more room for bargaining and a much better chance that I'll be able to buy at a lower price. Remember that as a buyer, you always have the opportunity of walking away and coming back at a later time. True, you might lose the property to another buyer, but if the property is likely to be sold immediately, then you will simply have to work a little faster. In such an event, you can still walk away after putting a one- or two-hour time limit on your offer and leaving a phone number. Then go back to your motel room, or go back home and wait. If no call is forthcoming within the time limit, wait an extra half hour, and if you still want the property, come back with a higher counter-offer or agree to his or her price.

No matter how you work your purchase program, don't simply accept the seller's price. Try to bargain and try to start the normal dickering process at a low price. The seller will usually counter with a small reduction of his or her original asking price, then the buyer comes back with another counter-offer, a little bit higher this time, the seller comes down a little bit, the buyer goes up, the seller comes down, and finally a price is reached. In the haggling process, remember that price may not be the only consideration. There may be other items involved. There might be better terms arranged; there may be farm equipment that might be thrown into the deal; there could be furnishings in a house that is on the property that might be included; there might be a better easement across some other land that the seller isn't selling; there might be services performed by the seller, for example, if he's in the business of drilling wells or he's in the construction business; different values could be added to the deal to make it sweeter for the buyer to buy or the seller to sell.

Remember to always get into a bargaining posture. Do not walk into a deal feeling that you're going to insult the seller by countering. Many times the seller or broker will be sitting with a piece of property that is a bit high priced, and not getting many bids on it. He or she would be more than delighted to have someone come and make an offer so that the bargaining process could be started and they could finally sell that piece of property. In essence, you're doing the seller a favor by making an offer, no matter how low that offer is. By the way, if you're dealing with a broker, remember that the broker *must* present all bona fide offers to the seller, so don't let the broker talk you out of a low offer; make him or her present it.

Once you have agreed on the price, make certain the terms are spelled out in any written offer you sign. Be careful to write in any and all terms you want as part of your offer, because once you've signed it, you're committed, and verbal promises or changes probably won't be honored. Although it probably won't be accepted, try (during the bargaining process) to make your offer verbally and see if you can get a reaction from the broker or the seller. A foolish broker or seller will react. However, a smart broker, one who is doing his or her job properly, will insist that your offer be in writing and accompanied by some sort of deposit or good-faith money to show that you earnestly do mean business. If a broker or seller accepts a verbal offer and responds to it, it's usually an indication that he or she is very, very anxious to sell. In such a situation, you should consider offering an extremely low price when you do get around to the written offer.

As to your deposit, in some cases there are specific rules with regard to how much of a deposit is necessary, such as in the case of the VA or FHA, but barring such guidelines, a deposit of five to ten percent is usually acceptable.

When you make an offer to a broker, he or she will usually have you sign an "Offer to Purchase" or an "Agreement to Purchase" (you'll find samples under the "Forms" appendix in the back of this book). The agreement will lay out all the basic terms and conditions of the sale, without going into the details that are handled at the closing. At this point, you want to be sure to cover all the different aspects that you're going to be concerned with, such as:

1. If you're not buying the property for cash, and the seller is willing to finance, make certain the terms are fully spelled out.
   a. Amount of the down payment.
   b. Balance due.
   c. Annual interest rate.
   d. Whether the payments are to be paid monthly, annually, quarterly, semi-annually, principal once a year, interest twice a year.
   e. If an option payment was involved, did you deduct it from the price?
   f. What are the release provisions?
   g. When does title pass?
   h. When can you take possession?
2. Do you want to make a final inspection prior to closing?
3. Is the seller the sole seller or are others involved?
4. The title search.
5. The time period for accepting the offer.
6. Termite inspection of all domiciles.
7. Who will hold earnest money?
8. Amount of earnest money.

9. If you have to get bank financing, the financing clause.
10. If property is not surveyed, who will pay for survey?

Make certain that your offer is subject to any and all conditions you want to put in. Remember to include a specific short period for the seller to accept the offer. If you make an offer and don't put a time limit in, the seller could use your offer as a wedge to get other possible buyers to raise their prices, so a period of one, two, or three days is more than sufficient for the seller to either accept or reject your offer.

Lastly, you must specify the date of the closing, so that it isn't put off too far. Be sure to include any other provisions that you want as part and parcel of the sale. As far as the law is concerned, if something isn't written down in a real estate transaction, it does not exist.

At this point, you will be required to put up your earnest money or deposit. Normally, this money (if you are dealing with a licensed broker) will be held by that broker in a separate and distinct account called an escrow account. It will be held there until the transaction is finished. In most states, the money, by law, not only must be held in a separate account but it can't be intermingled with other monies of the broker or anybody else.

There is another way to tie land up without an agreement of sale, and that is an "option." An option simply means that you buy the right to buy the land at a later date at a specific price. An option is usually taken for any number of days, weeks, months, but rarely more than a year, unless it's a long-term option, which is something we're not concerned with here. There can be numerous reasons for wanting to option land before buying it. Possibly you don't have enough money to buy the land, but you don't want to risk the land being sold to somebody else, so you risk a small amount of money for the privilege of delaying your decision to buy. Such a delay gives you time to see some of your friends and see if they may want to buy in with you and share the cost, or more time to investigate the property (especially if it's a large tract) and make your mind up. So what you do is option the land. Look up the Option Form on page 131. It is a relatively simple form to fill out. Basically, you pay the seller a sum of money. The amount is decided by you or the seller. It could be $500 or $5,000, it could be five or ten percent of the purchase price—any amount that you both decide on—for the right of taking the property off the market and tying it up at a specific price until a specific date.

The amount that you pay for the option can be included as part of the earnest money or part of the final deal, or it could possibly be held totally apart from the final sale; that's between you and the seller. The three elements of the option are: the amount you pay for the right to hold the land off the market, the exact sale price at which you are going to buy it, and the date at which your option expires. An important thing to remember (especially if you're not dealing with a licensed broker or real-estate salesperson, but possibly with the owner of the property or his or her agent) is to make certain that the option forms you're signing are viable and will hold up legally if anything should happen. The way to do that, of course, is through the advice of an attorney.

Whether or not you're dealing with a broker, get an attorney to assist you at the closing. Many people go to a closing and depend entirely on the directions of the seller's attorney. This is very foolish. No matter how honest that attorney is, he or she represents the seller, and will naturally look after the seller's interest first and foremost. An investment in your own attorney at a closing is a very smart move and may save you a great deal of grief. In most cases, the seller's attorney will draw up all the necessary papers, and usually there will be no problems, but it is always better to spend the little extra money that it's going to take and hire your own attorney. Have that person in on the closing to make sure that you're getting everything you deserve.

The closing should occur only after all the details are worked out, after the title search has been made, and after the insurance and property taxes have been prorated. If you're buying the property in the middle of the year, and the insurance has been paid, then it's proper for you to repay the seller for the amount of insurance premium which is going to cover the period that you're going to own that property. The same applies to the taxes. If, let's say, you're buying the property on February 1, then, at the end of that year, the previous owner is going to get the tax bill because he or she owned the property on January 1. Usually the seller will forward that tax bill to you even though technically it is not your obligation to pay it even though you owned the property for 11 months out of that tax year. In the closing, the seller will pay you for one month's tax obligation, so that when you get the tax bill you can pay it in full. In the closing you will also prorate the costs of other things, such as any stocks of fuel oil, coal, wood, or any fuel that you will be using. The amount that is left should be prorated so the seller gets paid back for the amount remaining for your use.

When a bank or a savings and loan is involved, there is usually something called "points" involved in the loaning of the money. This is a service charge that the financial institution charges for processing a loan. By points, they mean a percentage of the loan. Say you're taking out a loan of $50,000, one point (1%) would be $500. That would possibly be their fee for handling the paperwork. Basically, in a closing the buyer pays for the property, a proration on the insurance, possibly the real estate taxes, the legal closing costs, the title search, and possibly some miscellaneous items.

The seller usually takes care of the revenue stamps, the preparation of the deed, and the taxes involved in the actual transaction. The points of the loan discount could be paid by either one, dependent upon the agreement, but they are usually paid by the borrower (buyer). It is usually best to have the attorneys take care of the closing. They're well versed in this area, they know what to do, they know what to look out for, so it is almost an automatic process for them. The charge usually will be well worth the result.

Now the transaction is over and the long process is ended—almost—and you're the proud owner of that piece of property that you've always wanted. Your first question is "What do I do now?" Well, that is really divided into three areas: (1) What do I do immediately? (2) What do I do in the not-too-distant future? (3) (*a little tagalong*) What do I do in preparation for the distant future?

The immediate, just as the other two, is dependent upon your wants and desires. If, for example, you have land that has a great deal of woodland, but you don't want people hunting on it, then the first thing you need to do is post your property in such a way that people will see that it's posted and notify the game warden that it's posted. If you intend to keep livestock, fence repairs and hay-storage facilities are going to be necessary. If you have any erosion problems on the property, take care of those just as soon as possible.

Nature will take over quickly if unchecked, as the growth in this gravel road shows.

This is the time to refer back to the notes you took during your in-depth investigation. Make a list of all the problems which need correction (the worst and most immediate first), then follow that list with another which encompasses all the things you intend to do with your property. If you can, put a timetable into this list. Be a dreamer if you must, but temper your dreams with the reality of time, money, and energy. And then, finally, start enjoying your land. After all is said and done, that's why you bought it.

13

BUYING SUBDIVIDED LAND

FROM A DEVELOPER

Among the large majority of honest real-estate salespersons and developers, there are, unfortunately, a few that are somewhat less than honest, and others who, although well-intentioned, are either undercapitalized or otherwise ill-prepared to build and run a successful development. It is for these reasons that you have to be especially careful when buying developed land. First of all, developed land will be considerably more expensive than "raw" land, simply because it has been developed. Someone has invested money, usually a great deal of money, in order to put in certain amenities, certain advantages, which will enhance the sale of the land. Those amenities can be anything, from a simple dirt road and a paper survey of the land, right up to and including swimming pools, tennis courts, and a country-club organization with apartments, condominiums, and townhouses. Buying or investing in structures such as townhouses or condominiums is entirely another matter; here we are concerned simply with the buying of land.

When you buy undeveloped land, you need to check everything out for yourself (as I've outlined in the first part of this book); hire an attorney to take care of the closing; and preferably work with a broker who knows the area and knows what he or she is doing. When you buy land from a developer, however, much of that checking out has already been done for you. In many cases, the developer has filed a Property Report with the Department of Housing and Urban Development (HUD), and is obliged by law to give you a copy. (HUD and Property Reports are discussed in full in the next chapter.) Such Property Reports will tell you a great deal about the development, but whether you get a Property Report or not, there are many facts you need to check out before you decide to buy from a developer.

In order to help you buy land with as little risk as possible, here are four guidelines. I have formed them into the word SAFE to make them easier to remember. They are basic rules you should follow *every time* you go through the land-purchasing procedure.

See the land. Inspect the property personally or, if that is impossible, have someone you trust inspect it for you.

Ask for a HUD Report. If none is available, find out why (you'll know how after reading the next chapter).

Find out all the facts. Use either the HUD Report or the evaluation form at the end of this chapter.

Evaluate all the information you have gathered. Take your time. Rushing quite often means trouble, because of overlooked problem areas. Take the necessary time to fully comprehend all the information you've gathered. If something is not crystal clear to you, get professional help from an attorney, real estate broker, or other land expert. Above all, be satisfied in your mind that the land you are buying suits your needs and desires.

As you get into the buying process, a variety of questions will come up which will need to be clarified. For example, how large will the development be when it is finished? If there is to be further expansion, where will the new lots go? Most developments have a map showing future projections; ask to see such a map. What you're looking for depends on your plans. For example, if you want a lot at the end of a cul-de-sac (a turn-around at the end of a road) so you won't have to put up with a great deal of traffic, you want to know that your peaceful turn-around won't eventually have a street extended through it.

You need to check on building and health restrictions. How strict are the county building codes? Are outhouses permitted? Are pets allowed? Check the set-back rules. How far back from the road, and how far in from each property line are you going to be allowed to build? What are the requirements for shed or room additions once you have built your original house, cottage, or cabin, or put in a trailer or motor-home pad?

Now you should start applying the P.L.A.N.E. Formula to the specific lot you like. First of all, is the price in line with similar lots in this development, as well as in other developments you've visited? (If not, why?) Be sure to get all the terms and conditions of the sale. Is there any prepayment penalty? If you pay on the lot for a year and suddenly get some extra money and want to pay off the lot, is there any penalty for doing so? Next, where within the development is the lot located? Is it in a high-traffic area? Is it on a particularly steep grade in the road? Is it located near the clubhouse and/or recreation complex? Access to a lot is usually not a problem in a recorded subdivision development because many county or state ordinances require the developer to provide good access. Since that's not always the case, check, and make sure the access into and onto your lot is not going to be unnecessarily difficult.

In a development, natural features are just as important as they are with the purchase of raw land. Topographically, how does your lot lie? Are you going to have to do a lot of excavating, draining, or a lot of fill work, in order to make the lot good enough to build on? In a development, the soil condition and the probability of percolation have probably already been checked by the

Health Inspector and approved through the subdivision ordinance, but you might check and make sure just to be safe. Some subdivisions still permit the use of outhouses; consider your feelings on that matter. Other subdivisions provide their own sewer systems and their own water hook-up, but will pass such costs on to you, either in higher lot costs or assessment fees. You're going to want to know about all such amenities. The more amenities and services, the higher the fee.

After you find out about all the existing amenities, ask what amenities are planned for the future. Such things as a clubhouse, tennis courts, a pool, fishing streams or a fishing pond may be planned. Ask which of these will be completed within the next six months, and what the projections are for completing the longer-range projects. Ask if the money to pay for future projects (ones that have not yet been started or completed) has been put into an escrow account—meaning, has the money been set aside specifically for that reason. This is very important, since a developer may sell your note to a third party who won't be responsible for completing the promised amenities. Let's say that the developer promises to build a pool, but before it's completed things turn sour and the developer has to sell the notes to a bank or another company. That bank or other company is not responsible for completing the pool. You may wind up either having to put up extra money to complete the pool, or not having a pool at all. You want to be very careful to make certain of what provisions there are for the completion of whatever amenities you're paying for.

There will be many other details you'll want to know. What waste disposal system will be used, septic tank, outhouse, or sewer hook-up? Will you have to drill a well? If so, what is the average depth of the wells, and what is the approximate drilling cost? What about garbage and trash collection? Another very important question is whether or not there is or will be a Property Owners' Association. Will there be a security system? How extensive? Will the roads have to be privately maintained and/or eventually turned over to the state? Will there be a clubhouse operation?

If you're going to have such services and amenities, they're going to have to be maintained and managed by someone. You want to find out who that someone is going to be. If the developer is going to continue to manage them, then you'll have to find out how much voice the property owners will have in the operation, and if, at any future date, the control of that operation is going to be turned over to the Property Owners' Association. In some cases it is, and in others it isn't, but know these facts before you buy, so you're not unpleasantly shocked later on.

One of the most important facts to find out is what restrictions or reservations are going to go on the deed. Most developers have at least some basic restrictions with regard to the kind and size of buildings you can build, cutting of certain trees, acceptable noise levels, and resale limitations. There are a variety of restrictions which can be put on lots, so you want to find out exactly what they are in order to make certain you don't object to any. This is a sample list used in one of the developments with which I am connected:

RESTRICTIVE COVENANTS

1. No business or commercial structures, including but not limited to hotels, motels, restaurants, stores, or amusement areas, shall be allowed.

2. All residence structures, whether houses, campers, tents, trailers, motor homes or mobile homes, etc., shall be constructed of conventional materials and shall be neat in appearance. No unsightly structures such as "tar-paper shacks" or converted buses shall be permitted. No permanent residences are permitted, except on certain specified lots. All structures will be set back 20 feet from any boundary.

3. Lots may not be redivided.

4. Septic tank systems or other waste disposal systems must be approved by the County Health Officials and may not in any way endanger any water supplies or waterways. All residences must have an acceptable sewage disposal system if they are to be occupied.

5. All the sites sold by the Developer will be subject to a monthly payment. *(This payment varies greatly from development to development, depending on facilities and services available at that development.)* It is payable in advance to the Developer or Property Owners' Association for the purpose of association operation, road maintenance, and property security. This service and charge will eventually be taken over by the Property Owners' Association. Said assessment will be enforced in law against the land, and acceptance of the deed for any of the said sites will constitute an agreement on the part of the purchaser thereof; his heirs, or assigns, to pay said assessment when due and that any unpaid assessment will be a lien on the purchaser's real estate.

6. No animals other than horses and those animals commonly known as household pets shall be kept on the premises.

7. No wood, timber, or trees may be cut for commercial purposes. No trees over 12 inches thick (at a point three feet above ground) may be cut by anyone without prior written approval of the Developer and/or Property Owners' Association, except for clearing of approved site or driveway.

8. No rocks, shrubs, or plants or other objects except those located on a purchaser's tract, may be removed except with prior written approval of the Developer and/or Property Owners' Association.

9. No gasoline-powered boats of any kind (models included) are permitted to operate in or on any streams, ponds, or lakes now existing or hereafter constructed, on the property.

10. No automobiles, automobile parts, household appliances, trash, garbage, or any other objects of any unsightly or useless nature may be discarded or abandoned on any homesites or anywhere on the property. Such property may be removed at the homeowner's expense.

11. All site owners acknowledge the right of the designated individuals to pass through this parcel on designated roadways and easements when such passage is necessary to install utility equipment or perform necessary services.

12. No motorbikes, motor scooters, lawn mowers, generators, chain saws, or other motorized items producing a noise level higher than a standard factory-equipped automobile shall be permitted anywhere on the property prior to 9:30 A.M. or after 9:30 P.M.

13. No open fires, trash incinerators, or open cooking pits (other than properly constructed charcoal broilers) shall be permitted anywhere on the property or homesites.

14. Invalidation of any one of these convenants by judgment or court order will in no way affect the other provisions which will remain in full force and effect.

15. The Developer shall have first refusal to purchase the lot of any owner who desires to sell same and has a purchaser ready, willing, and able to purchase said lot at the same sale price offered to the Developer, but this provision does not apply to any foreclosure sale under a Deed of Trust, and any foreclosure sale under a Deed of Trust shall be valid without first offering the property for sale to the Developer.

16. The streets will not be maintained by the Highway Department but will be maintained either by the Developer, as set forth in Restriction 5 above, or by the Property Owners' Association.

17. There will be no discharge of firearems within lots, nor hunting of any kind.

18. There will be no recreational motorbike riding within the lots.

Next, find out when you get the deed. Many developers sell land through what is termed a Land Contract. A Land Contract is strictly a legal document through which the developer promises to transfer ownership of the land and give you a deed only after you've made your final payment. If the contract is notarized when it is signed, you can take the contract down to the local courthouse and have it recorded. If you do that, it tells the world that you and the developer have a contract, so if anything happens to the developer, you will be on much safer legal ground. If the contract is not notarized when it is signed, then you cannot record it, and all you have is a contract between you and the developer which no one else is legally aware of. If that developer goes out of business, you won't be as secure as if you had a notarized contract, since the developer's creditors could take your lot or land as payment of the developer's debts.

For your own protection, if at all possible make certain that when you're buying land through a Land Contract, buy only through a contract that is notarized at the time of signing, so you can have the contract recorded. A recording fee usually runs anywhere from fifteen to fifty dollars, and is well worth your protection.

Usually, whether or not there is a Property Owners' Association, there will be maintenance charges to pay for the upkeep of everything from roads, the clubhouse, a swimming pool, to power lines. Such maintenance charges can run from very little money to a great deal. You want to find out exactly what those charges currently run, who has control of raising them, and who has the authority to spend that money.

The most sensible protection that you can have in purchasing land, as in the purchase of any other item, is good common sense. Nobody is going to give you something for nothing. If you want one of the better lots, you're going to have to pay a higher price than if you settle for one of the poorer ones. Keep in mind that a developer has to spend a great deal of money and take a lot of risk in preparing a development for sale. The developer is going to want a good return on his or her money. So the lots you buy in a development are usually going to cost a good deal more than land that is undeveloped. On the other hand, the fact that the land *is* developed usually makes it more valuable, and more likely to increase in value faster than raw land.

Always remember to be patient and to move slowly. Usually there are enough lots to go around. If you don't get the one you first picked out, you'll probably find one that will be just as nice, or perhaps you'll find another development that may be just as nice or nicer.

And finally, apply those final, basic questions: Does it really suit my needs? Is it what I really want? Is it going to make me happy? It's difficult to remember all the important points to ask about a land purchase, so I have prepared the following questionnaire to help you.

DEVELOPMENT CHECK-OUT QUESTIONNAIRE

Date _____

Name of development ____ *(NAME)* ____ Phone _____

Address of development _____

Name of developer (if different) ____ *(COMPANY)* ____

Address of developer (if different) _____

_____ Phone _____

How long in business? __ *12 YRS* __ When did development begin? __ *4 YRS AGO* __

_____ How many lots currently available? __ *536* __

How many lots planned in completed development? __ *750* __

What method of sale is used?
  1. Land Contract _____
     a. Is it notarized and recordable? _____
  2. Deed __ *✓* __
     a. Type __ *WARRANTY* __
     b. Any reservations? __ *HEAVY RESTRICTIONS ON RECORD* __
     c. Who records? __ *SELLER* __
  3. Other _____
     a. Explain _____

Is development land under a blanket mortgage? __ *YES* __
     If so, to whom? __ *(BANK)* __
What provisions for release? __ *AS LOTS ARE SOLD* __

Do gas, oil, mineral, and timber rights go to buyer? _NO_
    If so, which rights? _____
Are there any restrictions (list on back)? _YES_
Are there any easements? _UTILITY_
Is there a prepayment penalty? _NO_
Have the lots been surveyed? _YES_ Is the survey certified? _YES_
Has the subdivision plat been recorded? _YES_
Has the land been zoned? _NO_ Who pays the taxes? _BUYER_
How much yearly tax on lot? _44⁰⁰_ How much yearly tax on
association? _NONE_ What permits will I need? _BUILDING +
HEALTH_

Do I have legal access to my lot from a state road? _YES_
Are the roads complete? _NO_ If not, what is the completion date? _?_
How do I get the following?
    Water _DRILL_ Sewage disposal _SEPTIC TANK_ Gas _N/A_
Electricity _$5⁰⁰ MEMB. FEE +$52 INSTALL_ Phone _$15⁰⁰ FEE_ Removal of garbage _SELF_
How far is the closest of each of the following?
    Grocery store _12_ Gas station _4_ Town _12_ Hospital _12_
Police Station _12_ Fire Department _5_ Doctor _7_
Post Office _12_
Is there a Property Owners' Association? _FUTURE_ What are the dues? _250⁰⁰_
What do they cover? _ROAD UPKEEP AND CLUB FACILITY_
_____
Who controls the association? _(NOW) SELLER (IN FUTURE) BUYER_
What recreational facilities exist? _NONE_
What ones are planned? _DOCK, TENNIS COURT, POOL, CLUB HOUSE_
Is money in escrow to cover the unfinished recreational facilities? _NO_
Who maintains the recreational facilities? _SELLER, THEN BUYER_
_____
Are lots in the flood plain? _NO_ Any nuisances or deterrents? _NO_
_____
Any amenities? _NOTHING SPECIAL_
What actual costs will I have?
    Price of lot _10,000⁰⁰_ Finance charges _14%_ Property Owners' fee _250⁰⁰/YR_
Maintenance fee _____ Taxes _44⁰⁰_ Electricity _AS USUAL_ Sewer/septic tank
_750⁰⁰_ Water hook-up _350⁰⁰_ Gas hook-up _—_ Phone hook-up _47⁰⁰_
Other _____
_____
_____

Land such as this used to be sold over the phone to unwary buyers.

14

BUYING LAND FROM A

HUD REGISTERED DEVELOPMENT

The Office of Interstate Land Sales Registration (OILSR) is a part of the Department of Housing and Urban Development (HUD). Their primary involvement in the land-sales field is to see to the registration of certain land developments. One of HUD's primary responsibilities is to compel land developers to provide full disclosure of all pertinent facts concerning the sale of their land to all purchasers, and ample time for the purchasers to analyze that information before being obligated to buy. HUD's official address for all communications is:

Department of Housing and Urban Development
Office of Interstate Land Sales Registration
451 7th Street, S.W.
Washington, D.C. 20410

HUD's authority comes from the Interstate Land Sales Act of 1968. One of the main factors that spurred the passage of this law was that many people were buying land sight unseen. Fast-talking telephone salespersons, working out of so-called land "boiler rooms," literally talked hundreds of people into buying land, either by pitching it as an outstanding investment, or by using a variety of appeals based on empty promises. Many buyers plunked down their hard-earned money, and then found that most of the facts they were told and many of the promises that were made were simply not true. (This is why you should never buy land without thoroughly checking out all the facts, and never without actually seeing it and/or walking on it.)

Since HUD policies must cover a wide range of eventualities, the regulations which enforce the rules must be written in legally correct language, making it somewhat difficult for the average person to fully understand all the applications of these regulations. Indeed, as a land buyer (rather than developer) you don't necessarily need to know the detailed information of all the regulations, since many of them would not apply to your quest. The average residential land buyer needs to know:

1. Some basic general facts about buying land from a developer.

2. Whether or not the developer is exempt from registering with HUD, and, if not,

3. How to read and understand the Property Report you get from the developer and what to do with it.

(NOTE: If you wish to read the actual HUD regulations in their entirety, write or call HUD and ask them to send you any available information on land-buying regulations, especially Regulations No. 24 CFR, Parts 1700, 1710, 1715, 1720, and 1730.)

BASIC FACTS ABOUT BUYING LAND FROM A DEVELOPER

Know your rights as a buyer. Basically, what that means is to know what rights you have under the law and what protection you can get through HUD. HUD has the authority to take various punitive actions against developers who do not comply with their requirements. If, for example, a developer states certain promises in the Property Report and does not fulfill those promises (and you can prove it), many years after the signing of the contract, with HUD's backing you can force the developer to meet those obligations or get your money back, including interest, for everything you have paid in.

Know the developer. Learn as much as possible about the developer. If the developer is a company that you have never heard of, you'll want to check them out much more extensively than you would a company that has been developing land for 15 or 20 years and has an outstanding reputation.

Compare the facts. Make a comparison of the developer's supplied facts with those you can ascertain by using the procedures in the previous chapters of this book in relation to the HUD Report. Check out the actual lot by using as much of the P.L.A.N.E. Formula as is feasible, especially the "natural features" and "everything else" parts. Again, compare each item with the Property Report.

Know how to handle pressure sales. Know what you are doing when you encounter a high-pressure sales campaign. Buying land from a developer *strictly* as an investment is usually not a good idea (unless you are a highly informed and experienced land investor). There are, for example, many developers who will sell you a lot or tract, and then offer to rent it for you. They will give you the impression that the rental from the lot will cover your mortgage payment. This may well turn out to be true. There are developments in which this may happen, and where owners actually make money from such rentals. But there are others where it doesn't happen. You're going to have to use your good judgment to realize whether this is just a sales pitch. Most legitimate developments don't need to resort to high-handed or high-pressure sales tactics. If you do run into an overzealous or pushy salesperson, be careful.

In addition to the general informal guidelines listed above, HUD requires all nonexempt developments to file a "Statement of Record" with their office in

Washington, D.C., and to give each buyer or prospective buyer a Property Report. At the end of this chapter, you will find examples of two complete HUD Reports.

LEARNING IF THE DEVELOPER IS EXEMPT FROM REGISTERING WITH HUD

The only absolutely sure way to know is to write to HUD, giving them the name and the location of the development. However, there is a general rule you can follow. If a development has fewer than 100 lots, it is exempt. If it has more than 100 lots, and all those lots are larger than 20 acres, then it is also exempt. The exemption is from giving out a Property Report, but not from HUD's anti-fraud provisions. There are exceptions to the above rule, so don't use it indiscriminately.

SPECIFIC EXEMPTIONS

In the spring of 1979 and summer of 1980, new HUD regulations were put into effect which drastically changed land-registration requirements. The forms and format of the Property Report were changed, new safeguards were added, and different exemption rules were introduced. The two Property Report samples at the end of this chapter reflect those changes. I won't dwell on the pre-1979–1980 exemptions, because many of the developments existing at that time have either sold out or had to change over to the new format. However, if a development was exempt under old exemption rules, and, as of June 21, 1980, there were fewer than one hundred unsold lots in the development, then the old exemption was held in force, otherwise the new policies took hold. Under the new policies, these are the general exemptions which apply to a residential development, be it for permanent homes or resort property:

1. If a development meets any of the following criteria, it is totally exempt from all regulations:

    a. Any development with fewer than 25 lots.

    b. Any development selling land for commercial or industrial use.

    c. Any developments sold by any government body.

    d. Cemetery lots.

    (There are other criteria for exemption. See Note 1 below.)

2. If the development meets any of the following criteria, it is exempted from registration but still must meet HUD's anti-fraud provisions (see Note 2 below), which must be stated on the contract:

(NOTE 1) *There is a variety of other examples in these categories, but those listed are the most common. A complete outline of all exemptions is included in HUD Regulations 1710.5 through 1710.15.*

(NOTE 2) *The anti-fraud provisions are that the contract contain the following:*

    1. A legally sufficient and recordable lot description.

(Continued on page 72)

a. A development with fewer than 100 lots.

b. A development in which all lots are larger than 20 acres.

c. A development that sells less than 12 lots per year.

d. A scattered development in which each group of lots numbers less than 20.

HOW TO READ AND UNDERSTAND THE PROPERTY REPORT YOU GET FROM THE DEVELOPER AND WHAT TO DO WITH IT

Since the penalty for non-registration is fairly steep, you'll find that most developments that fall under HUD jurisdiction will be registered and will give you a Property Report. To make certain you understand what HUD means by certain terminology in the Property Reports, here is a list of definitions which you should review before reading a report.

Advisory opinion, the formal, written opinion of the Secretary as to jurisdiction in a particular case or the applicability of an exemption under 1710.5 through 1710.15, based on facts submitted to the Secretary.

Agent, any person who represents or acts for or on behalf of a developer in selling or leasing, or offering to sell or lease, any lot or lots in a subdivision. This term does not include an attorney-at-law whose representation of another person consists solely of rendering legal services.

Available for use, in addition to being constructed, the facility is fully operative and supplied with the materials and staff necessary for its intended purpose.

Beneficial property restrictions, restrictions which are enforceable by the lot owners and are designed to control the use of the lot and to preserve or enhance the environment and the esthetic and economic value of the subdivision.

Blanked encumbrance, a trust deed, mortgage, judgment, or any other lien or encumbrance, including an option or contract to sell, or a trust agreement, affecting a subdivision. This term does not include any lien or other encumbrance arising as the result of the imposition of any tax assessments by any public authority.

Common promotional plan, a plan undertaken by a single developer or a group of developers acting together to offer lots for sale or lease; land, offered for sale by a developer or group of developers acting together, that is contiguous or is known, designated, or advertised as a common unit or by a common name. Such land is presumed, regardless of the number of

2. *A statement that the seller will give the buyer written notification of the buyer's default or other breach of contract with at least 20 days to correct that default or breach.*

3. *Notice that if the buyer does lose rights in a lot after more than 15 percent of the principal has been paid in, the seller shall refund to the buyer any amounts of the principal in excess of the 15 percent after deducting any legal fees and other damages.*

lots covered by each individual offering, to be offered for sale or lease as part of a common promotional plan.

Date of filing, means the date a Statement of Record, amendment, or consolidation, accompanied by the applicable fee, is received by the Secretary.

Developer, any person who, directly or indirectly, sells or leases, or offers to sell or lease, or advertises for sale or lease, any lots.

Good-faith estimate, an estimate based on documentary evidence. In the case of cost estimates, the documentation may be obtained from the suppliers of the services. In the case of estimates of completion dates, the documentation may be actual contracts let, engineering schedules, or other evidence of commitments to complete the amenities.

Interstate commerce, trade or commerce among the states or between any foreign country and any state.

Lot, any portion, piece, division, unit, or undivided interest in land, if the interest includes the right to the exclusive use of a specific portion of the land.

Offer, any inducement, solicitation, or attempt to encourage a person to acquire a lot.

OILSR, the Office of Interstate Land Sales Registration.

Owner, the person or entity holding the fee title to the land and having the power to convey that title to others.

Parent corporation, that entity which ultimately controls a subsidiary, even though the control may arise through any series or chain of other subsidiaries or entities.

Person, an individual, unincorporated organization, partnership, association, corporation, trust, or estate.

Principal, any person or entity holding financial or ownership interest of 10 percent or more in the developer or owner, directly or through any series or chain of subsidiaries or other entities.

Purchaser, an actual or prospective purchaser or lessee of a lot.

Rules and regulations, all rules and regulations adopted pursuant to the Interstate Land Sales Act, including general requirements.

Sale, any obligation or arrangement for consideration to purchase or lease a lot directly or indirectly. The terms "sale" or "seller" include in their meanings the term "lease" and "lessor."

Secretary, the Secretary of Housing and Urban Development or a duly authorized representative.

Senior Executive Officer, the individual of highest rank responsible for the day-to-day operations of the developer and who has the authority to bind or commit the developing entity to contractual obligations.

State, includes all the states, the District of Columbia, the Commonwealth of Puerto Rico and the territories and possessions of the United States.

Start of construction, breaking ground for building a facility, followed by diligent action to complete it.

Subdivision, any land which is located in any state or in a foreign country and is divided or proposed to be divided into lots, whether contiguous or not, for the purpose of sale or lease as part of a common promotional plan.

Since the purchase of land involves many detailed points of law not commonly known to the average person, the purpose of a HUD Property Report is to guide the potential buyer of land in a relatively large development through the maze of legal aspects, purchase procedures, and the normally unforeseeable (for the average person) situations encountered in the land transaction. Used properly, a HUD Report advises on the various aspects of the purchase procedure, potential pitfalls, possible problem areas, what's expected of the buyer, what the developer promises to do, and when the developer promises to do it.

You are given ample time to analyze the Report and to take it to and discuss it with a lawyer, a real-estate broker, or some other knowledgeable person who can explain any parts of the report which you may not fully understand. When the older form of the report was in effect, you had up to 48 hours to read over the report and, if you desired, turn your contract back in for a full refund. The new rules give you a minimum of seven days, up to a maximum of two years, depending on the conditions at the time you signed the contract.

Although the following two sample Property Reports aim at accomplishing the same end, they are considerably different in form and format. The current Property Report form is a major improvement over the old one. It is much more complete in its coverage and much clearer in its explanations.

During the purchase process, you should receive a copy of the Property Report before you sign anything. When you receive the Property Report, you must sign a duplicate page of the Report to show that you received it. That signed page stays with the developer as proof. After you signed for the Property Report, you can then sign the Contract of Sale (remember you have at least seven days to rescind it). Before you leave the development, read and study the Report carefully. Check out as many points covered by the Report as possible. See any physical comparisons by driving through the development again (with or without the sales representative).

Once you are satisfied that the various physical aspects check out, go back to the office and review any points that are not completely clear to you. When you get home, read the Report again and mark any items you still don't fully understand. Then make arrangements to meet with some expert (lawyer or other) to have them explained. And finally, *do not throw the report away*. File it away with the other important papers of the transaction. You may wish to use it for reference many years from now.

Should you decide to cancel the contract within the allotted time period, call the developer's office. Then send them a letter (use the form in the new Property Report), saying you wish to cancel the sale. Be sure to send it by certified mail. If they don't refund all your money within a reasonable length of time, contact HUD.

PROPERTY REPORT TYPICAL OF THE TYPE USED PRIOR TO THE SPRING OF 1979

The following Report may still be in use today by those developments in existence prior to the spring of 1979. In reading over the Report, keep in mind that it is simply a sample, and that the actual Report you see may contain information somewhat different from this Report. In explaining the various points, I have tried to be as brief as possible, while still attempting to explain the essential meaning of each point. If some points still seem unclear to you after you have read them several times, check with an attorney, a real estate broker, or other knowledgeable person who can assist you with the explanation.

The cover sheet of the HUD Property Report needs to be signed, filled in at the bottom, and left with the developer. Make certain that you have received the HUD Report before you sign anything. By signing this cover sheet, all you're doing is signing recognition that you have received the HUD Report. You are not waiving your rights to anything.

PROPERTY REPORT

NOTICE AND DISCLAIMER

BY OFFICE OF INTERSTATE LAND SALES REGISTRATION

U.S. DEPARTMENT OF HOUSING AND URBAN DEVELOPMENT

The Interstate Land Sales Full Disclosure Act specifically prohibits any representation to the effect that the Federal Government has in any way passed upon the merits of, or given approval to this subdivision, or passed upon the value, if any, of the property.

It is unlawful for anyone to make, or cause to be made to any prospective purchaser, any representation contrary to the foregoing or any representations which differ from the statements in this property report. If any such representations are made, please notify the Office of Interstate Land Sales Registration at the following address:

Office of Interstate Land Sales Registration
HUD Building, 451 Seventh Street, S.W.
Washington, D.C. 20410.

Inspect the property and read all documents. Seek professional advice. Unless you receive this property report prior to or at the time you enter into a contract, you may void the contract by notice to the seller.

Unless you acknowledge in writing on a waiver of purchaser's revocation rights form that you have read and understood the Property Report and that you have personally inspected the lot prior to signing your contract, you may revoke your contract within 48 hours from the signing of your contract, if you received the Property Report less than 48 hours prior to signing such contract.

1. NAME(S) OF DEVELOPER:
2. NAME OF SUBDIVISION:
   LOCATION:
2a. EFFECTIVE DATE OF PROPERTY REPORT:

IMPORTANT—READ CAREFULLY

Name of Subdivision:

By signing this receipt you acknowledge that you have received a copy of the property report prepared pursuant to the Rules and Regulations of the Office of Interstate Land Sales Registration, U.S. Department of Housing and Urban Development.

Received by: _____
Street Address: _____
Date: _____
City: _____State: _____
Zip: _____

Notwithstanding your signature by which you acknowledge that you received the Property Report you still have other important rights under the Interstate Land Sales Full Disclosure Act.

2b.
(This number refers to the number of lots at the time the developer submitted the report or at the time of the update. It does not necessarily reflect the total number of lots in the development at the time you're buying, or the total number that will eventually be in the development.)

3. List names and populations of surrounding communities, and list distances over paved and unpaved roads to the subdivision.
(Refers to the distances to the nearest towns and cities on both paved and unpaved roads.)

4a. Will the sales contract be recordable? Yes or no?
(Informs you whether or not the installment contract will be recordable. If you

are to be fully protected by law, you must record your contract. The contract must be notarized at the time of signing. If the contract is not notarized, it is not recordable.)

4b. In the absence of recording the contract or deed, could third parties or creditors of any person having an interest in the land acquire title to the property free of any obligation to deliver a deed? Explain.

(Points up the fact that if you do not record your land contract, then a creditor or a third party could come between you and your land because you have not published [recorded] the fact that you have bought it.)

4c. State whether and/or when the contract or deed will be recorded, and who will record it. State who will bear the costs of recordation, and the amount if those costs are to be borne by the purchaser.

(Specifies who has the obligation of recording the contract. Although it is the obligation of the buyer, the developer will sometimes record it for you; you still pay the costs. Those costs, as stated earlier, can run anywhere from ten or fifteen dollars on up to fifty dollars, or even more in some states.)

4d. What provision, if any, has been made for refunds if buyer defaults? If none, and the buyer's payments are to be retained, state whether his loss will be limited to the amount of his payments to date, or whether he will be responsible to the developer or his assignees for additional damages or for the balance of his contract.

(Specifies what happens to the money that a buyer has put in if the buyer stops paying on the purchase of the lot. In most cases, in a development this money is simply forfeited by the buyer, used as liquidated damages, and kept by the developer.)

4e. State prepayment penalties or privileges, if any.

(States if there are any penalties for early payment. In other words, suppose you buy a lot and you pay twenty percent down, and then you pay for another year. You then decide to pay the balance off at once, instead of continuing to pay on time. In some cases, there will be a penalty for doing this, because the developer is losing income from interest if you pay early.)

5. Is there a blanket mortgage or other lien on the subdivision or portion thereof in which the subject property is located? Yes or no? If yes, list below and describe arrangements, if any, for protecting interests of the buyer if the developer defaults in payment of the lien obligation. If there is such a blanket lien, describe arrangements for release to a buyer of individual lots when the full purchase price is paid.

(An extremely important part of the HUD Report, because it tells you whether the land that you are buying is owned by the developer free and clear, or if the developer is buying it "on time" and has the land you are buying mortgaged with a lender. If the developer does not owe anything on the land, then the word "no" will appear, and you will have no concern. If the word "yes" appears, check the next paragraph to find out what kind of arrangements were made in case the developer does not pay his mortgage.

Let's say, for example, you're one of the first purchasers in a development which is selling mortgaged land. If the developer, for some reason, goes broke, then the bank or lender which is holding the mortgage on the entire piece of property repossesses the land and becomes its owner. You might have to make some sort of arrangements with that bank in order to keep your land, since the bank or lender would not necessarily be obligated to honor your contract with the developer.

In many cases, the developer will have an agreement with the person holding the large mortgage to release the pieces of land that are sold by the developer to a person like yourself. Unfortunately, those releases are usually in larger tracts than one or two lots, so even when releases are stipulated, there is sometimes a period of time in which you do run the risk of losing your land while the developer accumulates enough sales to release the larger tract which contains your lot. Here is where dealing with a reputable developer really makes the difference. Don't be scared away from buying in a development where this lien situation exists. It probably is the case in most developments. Simply weigh the risks against the benefits, and carefully review the developer's financial statement. Go to an accountant if necessary.)

6. Does the offering contemplate leases of the property in addition to, or as distinguished from, sales? Yes or no? If yes, a lease addendum must be completed, attached, and made a part of the property report.

(Deals with leasing [renting] land in the development, rather than buying it. If you're investing money in a piece of property, you want to know if the land next to you can simply be leased. If so, the people who lease it will not be owners—they'll be renters—and may act differently from the way you would act as an owner.)

7. Is buyer to pay taxes, special assessments, or to make payments of any kind for the maintenance of common facilities in the subdivision (a) before taking title or (b) after taking title? If yes, complete the schedule below:

(Tells you who pays taxes or special assessments for common facilities, such as roads, clubhouse, swimming pool, etc., when those taxes have to be paid, and how much each tax or assessment is going to cost you.)

8a. Will buyer's down payment and installment payments be placed in escrow or otherwise set aside? Yes or no? If yes, with whom? If not, will title be held in trust or in escrow?

(Asks whether the money paid as a down payment, along with the monies paid in over the years, will be set aside in a special escrow account until the deed is turned over. In most cases the answer is no, the money is not held in escrow, the money is simply spent as the developer sees fit.

It also asks if the money is not set aside, if the title to the land is put in trust or in escrow. Again, usually the answer is no, it is simply held by the developer until full payment is made. This is especially true where the developer is borrowing money on the land and where there is a Deed of Trust against the land, because if the ownership is in the developer during all those years, the developer does not need to release the land, and can use the money on other things.)

8b. Except for those property reservations which land developers commonly convey or dedicate to local bodies or public utilities for the purpose of bringing public services to the land being developed, will buyer receive a deed free of exceptions? Yes or no? If no, list all reservations and their effect upon buyer.

(Asks if the title as given over in the deed is free of exceptions other than normal utilities easements. In most developments the answer will be no, because there are restrictive covenants [restrictions] in the development; the deed will specify or refer to those.)

8c. List the permissible uses of the property based upon the restrictive covenants, and which are consistent with local zoning ordinances.

(Specifies the kind of dwelling that can be put on the properties. Naturally, if you're buying a piece of land and want to put up a beautiful mountain cabin, you probably don't want to be next to a mobile-home park or a multi-family dwelling where there will be apartment units that won't be compatible with your home.)

8d. List all existing or proposed unusual conditions relating to the location of the subdivision and to noise, safety, or other nuisances which affect or might affect the subdivision.

(Simply asks about any possible detriments. For example, is there excessive noise nearby, are there any offensive smells, are there any unusual safety hazards, and what is the potential for fire or flood?)

9. List all recreational facilities currently available, proposed, or partly completed (e.g., swimming pools, golf courses, ski slopes, etc.), and complete the following format for each facility:

Facility	% Complete	Estimated Completion Date	Financial Assurance of Completion	Developer Obligated?	Buyer's Cost or Assessments

State who will own the facilities.

(Requires the listing of all recreational facilities, both existing and promised. If they are not finished, then requires an anticipated date of completion; asks what assurance the developer gives of their completion; if money has been set aside for the facilities; and all the details with regard to fulfilling the promises that were made. Remember that if the developer goes out of business before these facilities are completed, the people who foreclose on the developer are not obligated to finish these facilities.)

10. State availability of the following in the subdivision: State any estimated costs or assessments to buyer or lessee. If only proposed or partly completed, state estimated completion date, state provisions to assure completion, and give an estimate of all costs to buyer or lessee, including maintenance costs.

10a. Roads:

1. Access:
   Paved
   Unpaved
2. Road system within the subdivision:

(Specifies the types of roads that are available to and throughout the development, their condition, and whether they are paved or unpaved.)

10b. Utilities:

1. Water:
2. Electricity:
3. Gas:
4. Telephone:
5. Sewage disposal:
6. Drainage and flood control:
7. Television:

(Refers to the availability and status of utilities, such as water, electricity, gas, telephone, sewage, along with flood control and television reception.)

10c. Municipal services:

1. Fire protection:
2. Police protection:
3. Garbage and trash collection:
4. Public schools:
5. Medical and dental facilities:
   i. Hospital facilities:
   ii. Physicians and dentists:
6. Public transportation:
7. U.S. Postal Service:

(Refers to municipal services, if they exist, what kind they are, and how far away they are located.)

11. Will the water supply be adequate to serve the anticipated population of the area?

(Asks if there is enough water in the area to supply the needs of the proposed population of the development. If the answer is no, find out why, and what will be done to bring in enough water.)

12. Is any drainage of surface water, or use of fill necessary to make lots suitable for construction of a one-story residential structure? Yes or no? If yes, state whether any provision has been made for drainage or fill, and give estimate of any costs buyer would incur.

(Asks if there is any standing water or if fill would be necessary to make building possible, or if there are any costs to the buyer to make the land usable.)

13. State whether shopping facilities are available in the subdivision; if not, state the distance in miles to such facilities and whether public transportation is available.

(Deals with shopping facilities on the property or near it, and what kind of public transportation is available.)

14. Approximately how many homes were occupied as of September 1, 1976?
(Deals with the number of homes existing at the property at a specific date.)

15a. State elevation of the highest and lowest lots in the subdivision and briefly describe topography and physical characteristics of the topography.
(Refers to the elevation. If you suffer from heart disease or high blood pressure, you want to pay particular attention to this figure.)

15b. State in inches the average annual rainfall and, if applicable, the average annual snowfall for the subdivision of the area in which it is located.
(Will give you the rainfall and snowfall averages. Here again, if you're asthmatic or have medical problems that tend to be aggravated by humidity, such as arthritis, then you want to pay particular attention to this figure.)

15c. State temperature ranges for summer and winter, including highs, lows, and means.
(Gives you the mean temperature ranges. Again, health reasons may necessitate your checking this rather carefully.)

16. Will any subsurface improvement, or special foundation work be necessary to construct one-story residential or commercial structures on the land? Yes or no? If yes, state if any provision has been made and estimate any costs buyer would incur.
(Asks whether any special subfoundations need to be built. This may be necessary in swampy or sandy areas, where pilings have to be driven down to rock or a certain distance in order to provide proper foundation of a structure. If the land is in the mountains and is extremely steep, then some sort of scaffolding apparatus would have to be built in order to make building possible.)

17. State whether there is physical access (by conventional automobile) over legal rights-of-way to all lots and common facilities in the subdivision. State whether the access will be by public or private roads and streets and whether they will be maintained by public or private funds.
(Refers to legal access to the lot.)

18. Has land in the subdivision been platted of record? Yes or no? If not, has it been surveyed? Yes or no? If not, state estimated cost to buyer to obtain a survey.
(Refers to whether the subdivision has been platted and recorded. If it has, a map of the subdivision would have to be registered with the county. If the property has not been surveyed, the cost to you of such a survey must be shown.)

19. Have the corners of each individual lot been staked or marked so that the purchaser can identify his lot? If not, state the estimated cost to the pur-

chaser to obtain a survey and to have the corners of his lot staked or marked.
(Asks whether the corners of the lots have been staked and/or clearly marked. If they haven't, your cost for doing so must be shown.)

20. Does the developer have a program in effect to control soil erosion, sedimentation, and flooding throughout the entire subdivision? Yes or no? Describe the program, if any. Has the plan been approved or must the plan be approved by officials responsible for the regulation of land developments? Yes or no? Is the developer obligated to comply with the plan? Yes or no?
(Asks whether there is a soil-erosion control plan. Since many states require such a plan, the answer is often yes. The program needs to be described, explaining what measures, if any, will be taken by the developer, and whether or not the developer needs to comply with the program.)

21. State whether the subdivision is based on a proposed rather than a currently approved division of the land. If proposed, state whether the description of each of the lots in the offering is legally adequate for the conveyancing of the land in the political subdivision wherein the land is located.
(States whether or not the proper legal paperwork has been filed in order for the developer to legally convey the land that is being sold.)

22. State whether the subdivision must be approved by the local authorities before it is platted of record. If yes, and the subdivision plat has not been approved by the local authorities, or if the subdivision has not been platted of record, you are advised as follows: The local authorities may require significant alterations before they will approve the proposed use of the land. Zoning requirements may prevent the land from being used for the purpose for which it is currently being sold.
(States whether or not the development has been approved by a local board [such as a Planning Board or County Board of Supervisors] prior to the sale offer, and points out that such a board might make drastic changes in the development if prior approval had not been granted.)

23. State whether the developer is a newly formed entity. Yes or no? If yes, state the effect which the heavy expenditures necessary to begin a land development sales operation will have on the developer's earnings.
(Points out that if the developer is a new company, it will be facing heavy development costs. Since those costs would affect its first year's income, that expense could have a negative financial effect on the company.)

SPECIAL RISK FACTORS

a. The future value of land is very uncertain; do NOT count on appreciation.
(States that purchasing land within a development strictly for investment is not necessarily a good idea. It can be, but that decision is something you'll need to make after investigating all the facts. Always keep in mind that you must not assume that the land you're buying will increase in value.)

b. You may be required to pay the full amount of your obligation to a bank or other third party to whom the developer may assign your contract or note, even though the developer may have failed to fulfill promises he has made.

(Cautions that the developer has the right to sell your contract or assign the amount of money you owe him to a bank or to anyone else. That doesn't change the terms of your contract in any way. However, the new holder of the note is not required to fulfill any of the promises made by the developer which the developer did not finish. Therein lies the danger you face.)

c. Resale of your lot may be subject to the developer's restrictions, such as limitations on the posting of signs, limitations to the rights of other parties to enter the subdivision unaccompanied, membership prerequisites or approval requirements, or developer's first right of refusal. You should check your contract for such restrictions and also note whether your lien or any other liens on the property would affect your right to sell your lot.

(Simply stipulates that whatever obligations you agreed to when you purchased your lot transfer with the lot when you sell it. Be sure that you understand all the stipulations in your contract in that regard.)

d. You should consider the competition which you may experience from the developer in attempting to resell your lot and the possibility that real estate brokers may not be interested in listing your lot.

(Points up the logical fact that if, at the time you wish to sell your lot, the developer still hasn't sold out, then you and the developer obviously will be in competition with each other, a situation which may make it difficult for you to sell your lot.)

e. Changing land development and land use regulations by government agencies may affect your ability to obtain licenses or permits or otherwise affect your ability to use the land.

(Brings your attention to the point that a variety of government agencies, from the Health Department, Building Department, Soil Conservation Service, etc., could pass regulations which would affect the use of your land.)

FINANCIAL STATEMENTS

You should carefully review the attached financial statements of the developer. (See Exhibit A.)

(Name of Corporation)

By: _____
　　　　　　　　　　President

(A developer's financial statement must be attached. If you, the buyer, do not understand it, be sure to have an accountant go over it to see what kind of financial condition the developer is in.)

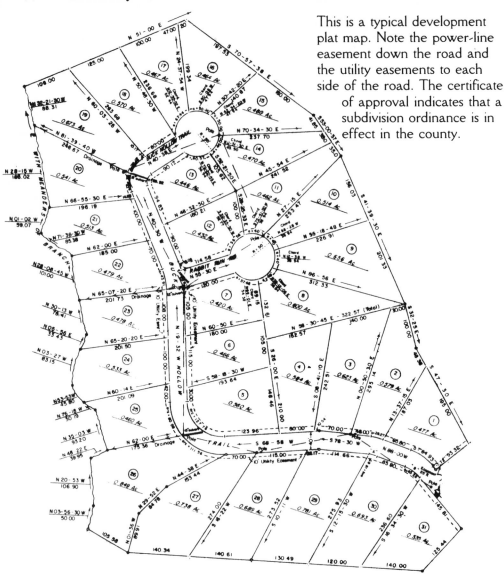

This is a typical development plat map. Note the power-line easement down the road and the utility easements to each side of the road. The certificate of approval indicates that a subdivision ordinance is in effect in the county.

NOTES

STREETS WILL NOT BE TAKEN OVER
AND MAINTAINED BY THE HIGHWAY DEPT
STREETS WILL BE THE RESPONSIBILITY
OF THE OWNER AND/OR PURCHASER AND
RECORDED IN EACH DEED

STREETS NOT DEDICATED TO PUBLIC USE
ALL STREETS TO HAVE 40' R/W

ALL PROPERTY BORDERING STREETS RUNS
TO CENTER OF STREET, EITHER PERPENDICULAR
OR RADIAL FROM CORNER ON R/W

MINIMUM BUILDING LINE TO BE 25 FROM
R/W LINE

IRON PIPES AT ALL CORNERS NOT
OTHERWISE NOTED

UTILITY EASEMENTS TO BE 20' ON EITHER SIDE
OF DASHED LINES SHOWN FROM POLE TO POLE
ACREAGE SHOWN DOES NOT INCLUDE THAT PORTION OF
ANY LOT WHICH LIES INSIDE THE R/W OF THE STREETS

NOTE APPROVED FOR VACATION OR INTERMITTENT
RESIDENCE ONLY NOT APPROVED FOR
PERMANENT RESIDENCE EACH LOT TO BE
EVALUATED BEFORE SEWAGE PERMIT APPROVED
OR DISAPPROVED

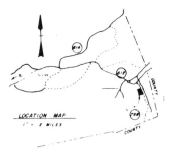

LOCATION MAP
1" = 2 MILES

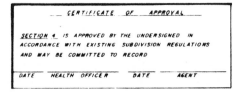

CERTIFICATE   OF   APPROVAL

SECTION 4 IS APPROVED BY THE UNDERSIGNED IN
ACCORDANCE WITH EXISTING SUBDIVISION REGULATIONS
AND MAY BE COMMITTED TO RECORD

DATE   HEALTH OFFICER   DATE   AGENT

PROPERTY REPORT TYPICAL OF THE ONE USED AFTER THE '79–'80 CHANGES

The new form of the HUD Property Report is much easier to understand and, therefore, needs much less explanation. There are several major differences between the new and old Reports other than simply the form. There are, for example, boxed warnings bringing your attention to possible trouble areas which may not be obvious by simply reading the Report. Another major difference is that the new report has a special duplicate certification and cancellation page at the end. One of the two sheets you sign and leave with the developer as proof that you received the Report. This special page also has a portion at the bottom which you can use to cancel your contract, thus saving you the necessity of writing a separate letter.

Another new page in the current Report is a cost sheet which outlines a variety of costs you may encounter during the sale or afterward. The new form of the Report has a table of contents, which makes it much easier for you to find information, and the risks of buying land are now located at the very front of the Report, rather than at the back, and are much more clearly stated.

The final major difference is the cover sheet. Firstly, you don't sign it. Secondly, the words printed in red, urging you to read this Report before signing anything, are clearly printed on the top half of the page rather than overprinted. The wording on this first page will also be different, according to the requirements at a specific development. For example, if the development was registered between the spring of 1979 and the summer of 1980, the 48-hour cancellation period will be in force. After June of 1980, you might find a variety of different wordings on the first page.

I have included the following two examples. Example A is the most standard form used. It permits cancellation up to seven days if you received a Report prior to signing the contract, and up to two years if you received it after signing the contract.

Example B carries the same two-year cancellation provision. However, in addition to its seven-day cancellation provision, an additional cancellation time has been added to meet any state law requirements. In this particular example, a six-month cancellation is given in addition to the seven-day cancellation if the buyer did not personally inspect the property. Time periods may vary, as may the requirements, so don't be surprised by a variety of different statements on the cover page.

The new-style Report has detailed explanations listed under headings, rather than answers to specific questions. It literally guides you, step-by-step, through the pertinent information you need to know to make a sensible purchase. On the *risks of buying land* page, you will now find much more clearly stated facts. Point two, concerning the completion of roads and utilities, may be deleted if all such amenities are completed prior to registration. I believe the remainder of the points are self-explanatory, as is much of the Report itself. If you carefully read through the glossary and use it while reading this sample Report, most, if not all, of its provisions will become quite clear. I have included a reference back to the first sample Report explanation as additional clarification.

Keep in mind that this is a sample Report. Since only general topics are used, the wording on the Report you receive may be considerably different. Again, if you have any questions on information within the Report on which you are still not completely clear, check with an expert. It will be money well spent.

READ THIS PROPERTY REPORT BEFORE SIGNING ANYTHING

This Report is prepared and issued by the developer of this subdivision. *It is NOT prepared or issued by the Federal Government.*

Federal law requires that you receive this Report prior to your signing a contract or agreement to buy or lease a lot in this subdivision. However, NO FEDERAL AGENCY HAS JUDGED THE MERITS OR VALUE, IF ANY, OF THIS PROPERTY.

If you received this Report prior to signing a contract or agreement, you may cancel your contract or agreement by giving notice to the seller any time before midnight of the seventh day following the signing of the contract or agreement.

If you did not receive this Report before you signed a contract or agreement, you may cancel the contract or agreement any time within two years from the date of signing.

NAME OF SUBDIVISION _____

NAME OF DEVELOPER _____

DATE OF THIS REPORT _____

_____

Example A

READ THIS PROPERTY REPORT BEFORE SIGNING ANYTHING

This Report is prepared and issued by the developer of this subdivision. *It is NOT prepared or issued by the Federal Government.*

Federal law requires that you receive this Report prior to your signing a contract or agreement to buy or lease a lot in this subdivision. However, NO FEDERAL AGENCY HAS JUDGED THE MERITS OR VALUE, IF ANY, OF THIS PROPERTY.

If you received this Report and inspected the property prior to your signing a contract or agreement, you may cancel your contract by giving notice to the seller any time before midnight of the seventh day following the signing of the contract or agreement. If you received this Report and signed your contract or agreement without an inspection of the property, you have six months from the date of signing the contract or agreement in which to inspect your lot and cancel your contract or agreement by notice to the seller.

If you did not receive this Report before you signed a contract or agreement, you may cancel the contract or agreement any time within two years from the date of signing.

NAME OF SUBDIVISION _____

NAME OF DEVELOPER _____

DATE OF THIS REPORT _____

Example B

TABLE OF CONTENTS

NOTE: In the Property Report, the words "You" and "Your" refer to the buyer. The words "We", "Us", and "Our" refer to the developer.

RISKS OF BUYING LAND

The future value of any land is uncertain and dependent upon many factors. DO NOT expect all land to increase in value.

Any value which your lot may have will be affected if the roads, utilities and all proposed improvements are not completed.

Resale of your lot may be difficult or impossible, since you may face the competition of our own sales program and local real estate brokers may not be interested in listing your lot.

Any subdivision will have an impact on the surrounding environment. Whether or not the impact is adverse, and the degree of impact, will depend upon the location, size, planning, and extent of development. Subdivisions which adversely affect the environment may cause governmental agencies to impose restrictions on the use of the land. Changes in plant and animal life, air and water quality and noise levels may affect your use and enjoyment of your lot and your ability to sell it.

In the purchase of real estate, many technical requirements must be met to assure that you receive proper title. Since this purchase involves a major expenditure of money, it is recommended that you seek professional advice before you obligate yourself.

-WARNINGS-
THROUGHOUT THE PROPERTY REPORT THERE ARE WARN-
INGS CONCERNING THE DEVELOPER, THE SUBDIVISION OR
INDIVIDUAL LOTS. BE SURE TO READ ALL WARNINGS CARE-
FULLY BEFORE SIGNING ANY CONTRACT OR AGREEMENT.

Property Report continues on the following pages

GENERAL INFORMATION

This report covers ___536___ lots located in *(County)*, *(State)*. See page _23_ for a listing of these lots. It is estimated that this subdivision will eventually contain _750_ lots.

The developer of this subdivision is:

(Corporation name, address, and telephone number)

Answers to questions and information about this subdivision may be obtained by telephoning the developer at the number listed above.

TITLE TO THE PROPERTY AND LAND USE

A person with legal title to property generally has the right to own, use and enjoy the property. A contract to buy a lot may give you possession but doesn't give you legal title. You won't have legal title until you receive a valid deed. A restriction or encumbrance on your lot, or on the subdivision, could adversely affect your title.

Here we will discuss the sales contract you will sign and the deed you will receive. We will also provide you with information about any land use restrictions and encumbrances, mortgages, or liens affecting your lot and some important facts about payments, recording, and title insurance.

METHOD OF SALE

Sales Contract and Delivery of Deed   At the time of your purchase, you will sign a purchase contract. Our deed will be delivered within 30 days from the date you sign the purchase agreement and pay to the sales agent the full purchase price or the full down payment if your purchase is financed by us. Also, if you finance the purchase price with us, you will sign a purchase money promissory note and deed of trust along with the purchase agreement. Our security on the balance of the purchase price will be the promissory note and deed of trust. In all events the purchase transaction will be completed and the deed delivered to you within 180 days from the date of your purchase agreement.

Type of Deed   The transfer of legal title will be accomplished by a general warranty deed.

Oil, Gas, and Mineral Rights   The oil and gas rights to the lots in this subdivision will not belong to the purchasers. The exercise of these rights could affect the use, enjoyment, and value of your lot.

ENCUMBRANCES, MORTGAGES, AND LIENS *(see part 5 of first sample report explanation)*

All the lots in the subdivision are subject to a blanket deed of trust in favor of *(Name)* Bank and Trust Company, *(Town)*, *(State)*.

Release Provisions   (see part 5 of first sample report explanation.) The deed of trust and supplemental release agreement, which are recorded in the *(County)* Register of Deeds Office, *(Town)*, *(State)*, contains a specific release provision. We will make arrangements with the bank to release your lot from the blanket deed of trust and will deliver to you a warranty deed, which is free and clear of any liens to you. Any expenses incurred in this process will be paid by us. We will obtain the release for your lot prior to the delivery of the warranty deed to you.

The release provisions for the deed of trust on the lots in this subdivision may be exercised only by us. Therefore, if we default on the deed of trust before obtaining a release of your lot, you may lose your lot and any money you have paid for it.

RECORDING THE CONTRACT AND DEED *(see part 4 of the first sample report explanation)*

Method or Purpose of Recording   Under *(State)* law, recording your warranty deed or the sales contract will protect you from future creditors of ours. Both may be recorded. We will record the warranty deed, but you will be responsible for recording the purchase agreement if you choose to have it recorded.

> UNLESS YOUR WARRANTY DEED OR INSTALLMENT SALES CONTRACT IS RECORDED YOU MAY LOSE YOUR LOT THROUGH THE CLAIMS OF SUBSEQUENT PURCHASERS OR SUBSEQUENT CREDITORS OR ANYONE HAVING AN INTEREST IN THE LAND.

Title Insurance   You should obtain an attorney's opinion of title or a title insurance policy which describes the rights of ownership being acquired by you. We recommend that you have the attorney interpret the opinion of title or the title insurance policy.

PAYMENTS

Escrow   You may lose your deposit, down payment and installment payments on your lot if we fail to deliver title to you as called for in the contract because they are not held in an escrow account which fully protects you.

Prepayment (see part 4E of first sample report explanation)   You may prepay any portion of your installment promissory note and deed of trust without penalty.

Default   If you default (such as failing to make your payment on your promissory note), we have no right against you. All we can do is declare the note in default and demand foreclosure under the deed of trust.

RESTRICTIONS ON THE USE OF YOUR LOT

Restrictive Covenants   Restrictive Covenants for the various sections of this development have been recorded in the *(County)* Register of Deeds Office.

A complete copy of these restrictions is available upon request. The major provisions of these agreements will be discussed in the paragraphs below. However, this discussion will only highlight certain areas of the covenants and should not be a substitute for a careful study of these agreements by you.

The only type of home permitted in this subdivision will be an individual site-built, single-family residence. The developer will specify floor-space requirements as well as architectural control and, therefore, has the right to approve building plans, placement on the lot, or the type of home or other building placed on the lot. This blanket authority extends to purely aesthetic considerations, such as type of building material on the exterior of the home, type of design of the home or other buildings, and decorative or privacy fences.

The convenants require approval for the cutting of any tree over ten inches in diameter at ground level and for the design and placement of the home and other improvements on the lot so as to blend with the surrounding terrain and natural cover.

The developer may initiate legal proceedings to enforce the provisions of the covenants.

These covenants are to remain effective until 2010 and may continue after that unless 55% of the owners wish to amend them some time thereafter.

Health Department regulations must be met in the use of the lots. Off-street parking is required. Dogs, poultry, and livestock are controlled, as are junk cars, unenclosed storage areas, clotheslines, fuel tanks and use of motorbikes or motorcycles.

The developer reserves the right to modify or amend these restrictions at its option so long as it does not alter the basic plan of development or the lots then making up the subdivision. Any modification will apply to every lot in the subdivision affected by such modification or amendment.

Easements   We have granted easements to *(Name)* Electric Corporation and to *(Name)* Telephone Company for the installment of electric lines and telephone lines from the main lines to each individual lot. However, these easements will not affect your use of the lot.

PLATS, ZONING, SURVEYING, PERMITS, AND ENVIRONMENT

PLATS

The subdivision plat has been approved by the *(County)* Planning Department. This plat has been recorded in the Office of the Register of Deeds for *(County)*, *(Town)*, *(State)*.

ZONING

No zoning regulations apply to the subdivision; however, restrictive covenants limiting the use of the lots in the subdivision have been recorded.

SURVEYING

All the lots being offered have been surveyed, staked, and marked for identification.

PERMITS

Prior to construction you must obtain a building permit from the *(County)* Tax Supervisor. You must also obtain a septic tank permit from the *(County)* Health Department before installation of the sewage system.

ENVIRONMENT

No environmental study has been prepared. No determination has been made as to the possible adverse effects the subdivision may have upon the environment and surrounding area.

ROADS

ACCESS TO THE SUBDIVISION

Access to the subdivision is provided by the roads listed below:

ROUTE NUMBER	SURFACE	WIDTH OF WEARING SURFACE	LANES
US 44	Asphalt	24 feet	2
SR 2447	Asphalt	20 feet	2
SR 4412	Asphalt	20 feet	2

These roads are public roads which are maintained by *(State)*. You will not be assessed for the maintenance costs incurred for these roads. No improvements to these roads are planned.

ACCESS WITHIN THE SUBDIVISION

Access from the subdivision entrance off SR 4412 to the lots in the subdivision is provided by 20-foot wide, two-lane roads. The rights-of-way for these roads are dedicated to the use of the lot owners.

We are responsible for construction of all interior roads. No portion of the construction will be borne by you.

-WARNINGS-
NO FUNDS HAVE BEEN SET ASIDE IN AN ESCROW OR TRUST ACCOUNT AND THERE ARE NO OTHER FINANCIAL ARRANGEMENTS TO ASSURE COMPLETION OF THE ROADS.

We have not fully completed the road system. However, we are committed to pay for all the construction costs to complete the road network. All roads within the subdivision will have a wearing surface of 20 feet and two lanes. The rights-of-way will be 60 feet in width.

ESTIMATED STARTING DATE (month/year)	PERCENTAGE OF CONSTRUCTION NOW COMPLETE	ESTIMATED COMPLETION DATE (month/year)	PRESENT SURFACE	FINAL SURFACE
2/80	70%	12/81	Sand	Marl

We are responsible for maintaining the streets until we form a Property Owners' Association. We will form a Property Owners' Association when we have sold out or substantially sold out our lots. The Property Owners' Association will then have the responsibility of maintaining the streets. During the period we are maintaining the streets, we will assess you for the street maintenance an estimated $50.00 per lot per year. The Property Owners' Association will also assess you for street maintenance; the assessment should be approximately the same as when we are maintaining the streets.

The table below identifies the distance (in miles) from the center of the subdivision to nearby communities.

NEARBY COMMUNITIES	POPULATION	DISTANCE OVER PAVED ROADS	DISTANCE OVER UNPAVED ROADS	TOTAL
(Town), (State)	800	18	0	18
(Town), (State) (County Seat)	2,500	14	0	14
(Town), (State)	200	12	0	12
(Town), (State)	2,000	14	0	14

UTILITIES

Here we will discuss the availability and cost of basic utilities. The areas covered will be water, sewer, electricity, telephone, as well as fuel and other energy sources.

WATER

Water will be obtained from private on-the-lot wells. The estimated cost of the system is $1,350.00. This will include drilling the well, the water pump, a small storage tank, installation, and hookup. There is no permit required for installation of a well.

The purity and chemical content of the water cannot be determined until each individual well is completed and tested. Should you be unable to obtain potable drinking water from an individual well on your lot, the contract provides for a refund of the money or exchange of the lot.

THERE IS NO ASSURANCE OF A SUFFICIENT SUPPLY OF WATER FOR THE ANTICIPATED POPULATION.

SEWER

The subdivision will use individual septic tanks rather than a central sewage system.

The *(County)* Health Department has granted general approval for the use of septic tank sewage systems. Your lot must be tested before the *(County)* Health Department will issue a sewer permit. If your lot passes approval, the Health Department in *(Town)* will issue a sewer permit without charge. The cost for the installation of a septic tank sewage system is estimated to be $600.00 to $900.00

THERE IS NO ASSURANCE PERMITS CAN BE OBTAINED FOR THE INSTALLATION AND USE OF INDIVIDUAL ON-SITE SYSTEMS.

Should you be unable to obtain a septic tank permit, your contract provides for a refund of the money or exchange of the lot.

ELECTRICITY

The *(Name)* Electric Corporation will supply electricity to the subdivision. The lines have not been extended to the individual lots but will be as and when needed, upon request. The electric company is responsible for construction of the electrical lines at no cost to you. To obtain electric service, a one-time membership fee of $5.00 is required.

TELEPHONE

Telephone service is available in the area through *(Name)* Telephone Company. Service lines have not been extended to the lots but will be as and when needed, upon request. The phone company is responsible for construction of the lines at no cost to you. The cost to you for telephone service is a one-time membership fee of $15.00 and an installation charge of $32.00.

FUEL AND OTHER ENERGY SOURCES

Electricity will be the only energy source in the subdivision.

FINANCIAL INFORMATION

A copy of our financial statement for the period ending September 30, 1979, is available from us upon request.

LOCAL SERVICES

In this category, we will discuss the availability of fire and police protection and the location of schools, medical care and shopping facilities.

FIRE PROTECTION

Fire protection is provided by the *(Town)* Volunteer Fire Department. This volunteer fire department provides year-round service at no cost.

POLICE PROTECTION

Police protection is provided by the *(County)* Sheriff's Office, located in *(Town)*. The access roads to the subdivision are patrolled by the *(State)* Highway Patrol.

SCHOOLS

You will be entitled to use *(County)* schools.
The nearest elementary and junior schools are located in *(Town)* and the nearest high school is located in *(Town)*. School bus transportation is available at the entrance to the subdivision.

HOSPITAL

The nearest hospital available to residents of the subdivision is the *(Name)* Hospital, located in *(Town)*. An ambulance service will be provided by the Volunteer Rescue Squad.

PHYSICIANS

There are physicians' offices located in *(Town)* and *(Town)*. Dentists' offices are located in *(Town)*.

SHOPPING FACILITIES

There are no shopping facilities in the subdivision. Shopping facilities are available in *(Town)*.

MAIL SERVICE

Currently, there is no mail service to each individual lot in the subdivision; however, mail will be delivered to a central pickup point at the entrance to the subdivision through the *(Town)* Post Office.

PUBLIC TRANSPORTATION

There is no public transportation from the subdivision to nearby towns. Furthermore, there is no public transportation system within the subdivision. Greyhound buses travel along U.S. 44 about 10 miles from the subdivision.

RECREATIONAL FACILITIES

FACILITY	PERCENTAGE OF CONSTRUCTION NOW COMPLETE	ESTIMATED DATE OF START OF CONSTRUCTION (month/year)	ESTIMATED DATE AVAILABLE FOR USE (month/year)	FINANCIAL ASSURANCE OF COMPLETION	BUYER'S ANNUAL COST OF ASSESSMENT
Boat Dock and Launch	0	9/81	4/82	None	⋆
Tennis Court	0	9/81	3/82	None	⋆
Swimming Pool	0	9/81	5/82	None	⋆
Club House	0	9/81	12/82	None	⋆

⋆The general assessment for all recreational facilities on an annual basis is estimated to be $250.00.

CONSTRUCTING THE FACILITIES

We are responsible for construction of all recreational facilities and we are contractually obligated to complete these facilities. You will not be required to pay any of the cost of construction of any of these facilities.

MAINTAINING THE FACILITIES

The maintenance of the facilities is currently our responsibility. In the future, these facilities will be conveyed to the Property Owners' Association. The Property Owners' Association will administer and maintain these facilities. We are contractually obligated to maintain these facilities.

PERMITS

The permits from the *(County)* Planning Department and the U.S. Army Corps of Engineers for the Boat Launch and Boat Dock have not been obtained; therefore, there is no assurance that the lot owners will be able to use the Boat Launch and Boat Dock.

WHO MAY USE THE FACILITIES

The facilities will not be open to use by the general public. The use of these facilities will be restricted to property owners and their guests.

SUBDIVISION CHARACTERISTICS AND CLIMATE

In this section, we will discuss the basic terrain of the subdivision, its climate and any nuisances or hazards in this area.

GENERAL TOPOGRAPHY

The subdivision is located on the Winding Way River near its outlet into the Atlantic Ocean. The lowest lot elevation is 20 feet and the highest is 40 feet. The land generally is sandy with gentle slopes and is covered with oak, pine, dogwood, and other native trees. The creeks and marshes in the subdivision comprise about 20% of the total land area within the subdivision and none of these areas will be developed.

All the lots in the subdivision have slopes of less than 20%. No special construction techniques will be required to erect a residence or place a manufactured home on the lot.

WATER COVERAGE

None of the lots in this subdivision are covered by water at any time during the year.

FLOOD PLAIN

The subdivision is not located in a flood plain. However, all the lots adjoining the Winding Way River and Happy Creek are in an area designated as flood-prone, specifically Lots 11–17, Lots 53–79, and Lots 98–112. Flood insurance is available for homes constructed in this area; the current cost of flood insurance is $125.00 per year. Flood insurance is required by lending institutions in the area.

FLOODING AND SOIL EROSION

We do not have a comprehensive plan to control soil erosion. Soil erosion could result in property damage and create a possible safety and health hazard.

NUISANCES

There are no nuisances which affect the subdivision.

HAZARDS

There are no hazards which affect the subdivision.

CLIMATE

The average temperature ranges, summer and winter, are contained in the table below. The average rainfall for this area is 51 inches; snow is rarely seen in the area.

	HIGH	LOW	MEAN
Summer	100	67	84.7
Winter	59	37.4	48.2

OCCUPANCY

No homes are occupied on a full-time or part-time basis in the subdivision as of February 2, 1980.

ADDITIONAL INFORMATION

Under this heading we will discuss the following areas:
1. The Property Owners' Association
2. The annual real estate taxes
3. Resale or exchange program
4. Equal opportunity in lot sales
5. Listing of lots

THE PROPERTY OWNERS' ASSOCIATION

There will be a Property Owners' Association, incorporated under the name of Happy Land Property Owners' Association, Inc. This association has not yet been formed but will be by us when we have sold out or substantially sold out our lots. We are responsible for forming the association. Once organized, we will retain no control over the association. Membership in the association, once it is formed, will be mandatory for all lot owners. The association dues will be set by its Board of Directors, who will be selected from amongst lot owners. The dues can be changed from time to time as deemed necessary by the Board of Directors.

Members could be subject to special assessments for repair of the streets, the lighting system, or the recreational facilities, if this should become necessary after the association takes title to these facilities.

The association once formed will be responsbile for the operation and maintenance of the streets, the lighting system, and all the recreational facilities. It will also have architectural control of all homes and other improvements placed on a lot and will have the right to enforce the restrictive covenants.

Prior to the formation of the Property Owners' Association, we will be responsible for the maintenance of the streets, the lighting system, and all recreational facilities. We will collect from you the assessments on an annual basis. We do not expect any increase in fees to maintain these services when we turn them over to the Property Owners' Association. We will turn the facilities over to the Property Owners' Association in good condition; and we expect the annual assessments to be sufficient to meet the Property Owners' Association's financial obligations, including operating costs, maintenance and repair costs, and reserves for replacement.

THE ANNUAL REAL-ESTATE TAXES

You will be responsible for *(County)* real-estate taxes commencing with the date of our transfer of the warranty deed to you. The current taxes for a lot assessed at $10,000.00 are estimated to be $44.00.

RESALE OR EXCHANGE PROGRAM

We have no program to assist you in the resale of your lot. Also, we have made no provisions for exchanging your lot, except if you are unable to obtain potable drinking water or a septic tank permit.

EQUAL OPPORTUNITY IN LOT SALES

We are in compliance with Title VIII of the Civil Rights Act of 1968. We have not, and will not, discriminate against you because of race, color, religion, sex, or national origin. Furthermore, we will not indicate a preference for, or a rejection of, any particular group in our advertising, rendering of lot services, or in any other manner.

LISTING OF LOTS

Lots 1–135 are recorded in Book 205, page 256, *(County)* Register of Deeds Office.
Lots 136–324 are recorded in Book 205, page 257, *(County)* Register of Deeds Office.
Lots 325–536 are recorded in Book 205, page 258, *(County)* Register of Deeds Office.

COST SHEET, SIGNATURE OF
SENIOR EXECUTIVE OFFICER

In addition to the purchase price of your lot, there are other expenditures which must be made. Listed below are the major costs.

All costs are subject to change.

Price of lot

Cash price of lot	$10,000.00
Finance charge *(5 YRS AT 12%)*	3,347.00
	$13,347.00

Estimated one-time charges

1. Installation of private well system	1,350.00
2. Installation of private on-site sewer system	750.00
3. Construction costs to extend electric and/or telephone services	None
4. Other	—
	$ 2,100.00

Total of estimated sales price and one-time charges $15,447.00

Estimated annual charges, exclusive of utility use fees

1. Taxes—average unimproved lot after sale to purchaser	44.00
2. Dues and assessments	250.00

The information contained in this Property Report is an accurate description of our subdivision and development plans.

_____
(Name)
President
Happy Land Corporation

RECEIPT, AGENT CERTIFICATION AND CANCELLATION PAGE
Fill in this sheet in duplicate—one stays with the developer

PURCHASER RECEIPT

IMPORTANT: READ CAREFULLY

NAME OF SUBDIVISION:
OILSR Number: Date of Report _____

We must give you a copy of this Property Report and give you an opportunity to read it before you sign any contract or agreement. By signing this receipt, you acknowledge that you have received a copy of our Property Report.

Received by ____ *(BUYER)* _____Date _____
Street address ____ *(ADDRESS)* _____
City _____State _____Zip _____

If any representations are made to you which are contrary to those in this Report, please notify the:

Office of Interstate Land Sales Registration
HUD Building, 451 Seventh Street, S.W.
Washington, DC 20410

AGENT CERTIFICATION

I certify that I have made no representations to the person(s) receiving this Property Report which are contrary to the information contained in this Property Report.

Lot(s) _____ *4 + 5* _____ Section _*II*_____

Name of salesperson _____ *GEORGE NIELSEN* _____

Signature _____ Date _____

PURCHASER CANCELLATION

If you are entitled to cancel your purchase contract, and wish to do so, you may cancel by personal notice or in writing. If you cancel in person or by telephone, it is recommended that you immediately confirm the cancellation by certified mail. You may use the form below.

Name of subdivision _____ *(NAME)* _____

Date of contract _____ *(DATE)* _____

This will confirm that I/we wish to cancel our purchase contract.

Purchaser(s) signature _____ Date _____

A breakwater made up of large chunks of concrete or large boulders is sometimes necessary to prevent beach erosion. A concrete or wood retaining wall at the edge of waterfront property permits more efficient use of the shoreline.

15

ENJOYING YOUR LAND

You are the only one who knows the real reason for your purchasing a piece of land. You are the only one who can determine the uses to which you're going to put that land, and exactly how you're going to enjoy it. Land, when it's intelligently purchased, always has been and probably always will be, a very sound and solid investment. But in order for that investment to be fruitful, it has to be bought "right." Hopefully, with the guidance of this book, you will be able to do just that.

Now there you are, sitting in the middle of your property, surveying your tiny, little, big, or monstrous estate and wondering, "What do I do next?" The answer to that question is totally dependent on your desires and your pocket-book. If you bought the land as an investment, then for many years to come you may well be doing only those things which are absolutely necessary.

You may wish to put in some foot trails to some of the more inaccessible areas. You may wish to thin out some of the timber, cut some of the under-brush, clean out some of the streams, perhaps put in a little dam, make a pond, put in some fish. There may be myriad different things you may wish to do to your new property.

However, there are probably some things that you may *have to do*. If, for example, you are faced with erosion problems (be they beach erosion or salt-water intrusion at the beach, run-off drainage problems on steep land or wind erosion in the desert or tundra), immediate corrective measures are necessary. If you have any attractive nuisances on your new property (such as ponds, lakes, or other features which kids might find attractive and on which or through which they might get hurt), then an insurance policy is an immediate requirement. If your purchase included any buildings or structures, fire and theft insurance may be needed.

Depending on your intentions, there are hundreds of possible actions you may have to take or may wish to take. At this point, the checklist you originally filled out on the property you now own will serve a further purpose by provid-ing you with the basic information to determine what actions you need or wish to take. Reread it carefully. This time look at the benefits as assets which you need to protect and at any corrective detriments as challenges that you need to surmount.

Be patient! As it was with buying your land, time is usually on your side. Hasty decisions almost always lead to grief. The pace and tempo of life is a bit slower outside the cities. That eternal "urban push" pressure is best left behind when dealing with country folk. Time has a way of getting stretched outside the city. Nine in the morning may oftentimes turn out to be more like ten or eleven in the morning; not because of uncaringness or carelessness, but because a neighbor may need help, or the tide may have to be "caught," or the hay has to be put up. City folk are not generally looked down upon, although many a tale has been told to suggest that they are. In the country, you are treated more or less as you treat.

Whether in the city or country, you'll usually find that government officials and officers are friendly and helpful, but always remember that you are playing in their pond. You may be a V.I.P. in your hometown, but don't try to act like one with them. Keep their needs in mind by trying to understand their motivations. You'll find you'll get a lot more accomplished. Do a little checking around to find out important events in their area and in their lives. If you're at the ocean, find out when the best local fishing occurs. Usually, the Building Inspector or the Health Inspector will take his vacation at that time. In the mountains, those same people will probably take a few days off at the start of trout season and again during hunting season.

Finally, make a list of the things you must do and the things that you wish to do with your property. The following is simply a guide, but it probably contains some of the items that you're going to be faced with:

1. Record all necessary papers immediately.

2. File all legal papers (originals) in a fireproof place (bank, safe-deposit box, or fireproof safe, etc.). Make copies to keep in a handy reference file.

3. Note any payment due dates. (Late payments cost you extra interest).

4. Make and file a list of names and addresses and phone numbers of all persons connected with the transaction.

5. Arrange to receive a publication which is likely to report news which might affect you and your land.

6. Sell or put up for sale any allotments or other saleable items or commodities on your property.

7. Clarify any questions or points that you are still hazy about with the proper people.

8. And lastly, take care of any physical needs on your property. For example, fertilization, water problems, erosion, brush removal, weeds, litter, fence repairs, dune rehabilitation and dune rebuilding, forest management, pollution, building repair, building removal, and any others.

After you have finished all the paperwork, have done all the checking, and have gone over all the lists, then just sit back and take a look at your property, and—no matter what reason you bought it for—start *enjoying* it, because, after all, that's the *real* reason you bought it.

Appendix 1

GLOSSARY

There are certain words that you really need to know while you read this book. You'll find them marked with an asterisk. I suggest you memorize these words and their basic meanings if you can. They will be of tremendous help when you are buying land. If you do run across a word in your land dealings that is not in this glossary, then I suggest that you either check with a good legal dictionary or a comprehensive total real estate dictionary, which you will most likely find at your local library.

ABANDONMENT   To surrender something forever without having any say as to who takes it over. (*When he left his farm, stopped making mortgage payments, and didn't pay the taxes, he was guilty of ABANDONMENT.*)

*ABSTRACT OF TITLE   A brief but complete history of the land, telling all the transactions (who bought and sold it, and if there are any claims against it), including everything that has happened to the land since it was first bought. An Abstract of Title is usually the result of a title search, conducted by a lawyer and traditionally paid for by the buyer. (*After the title search, the ABSTRACT OF TITLE showed that there were no liens against the property.*)

ACCELERATION CLAUSE   A statement, usually part of a Deed of Trust or mortgage, which says that the full amount of the loan toward purchase of land becomes due immediately if the property is sold or if the borrower fails to make installment payments at the proper time. (*When the house was sold, the lender was due the entire amount of the mortgage, due to the ACCELERATION CLAUSE. It therefore protected his interests.*)

ACCRETION   The buildup of soil or land on the shore or bank of a river or lake due to the change in the flow of the water. (*Due to ACCRETION, my property was enlarged by almost a fourth of an acre in just two years.*)

ACKNOWLEDGMENT   A formal statement or declaration before a notary or a duly authorized officer, attesting to the genuineness of a signature on a document. (*His signing of the deed is an ACKNOWLEDGMENT that he signed of his own free will and that the deed may be recorded.*)

ACQUISITION   An act of becoming an owner of something. (*His purchase of five acres down by the river was a very good ACQUISITION.*)

*ACRE   See *Measurements*.

*ACREAGE   Usually used to describe large tracts of undeveloped land. Acreage is also used to designate the amount of acres in a piece of land. (*I bought some good ACREAGE the other day, about 50 acres on a lake.*)

★ADJACENT   Lying close to or nearby, but not touching. (*My property is ADJACENT to Bill's, but Jerry's land separates us.*)

★ADJOINING   In actual contact with, actually touching. (*Our properties are ADJOINING; we have a common border on that old rock fence.*)

ADJUSTMENTS   Costs or charges which are divided between the buyer and seller at the time of closing a purchase of property. These include such things as taxes, interest, fuel, insurance, etc.

ADMINISTRATOR   A person appointed by the courts to handle the estate of a person who died intestate (leaving no will). (*I have been appointed ADMINISTRATOR of my uncle's estate since he never believed in writing anything down and died intestate.*)

AD VALORUM   Latin meaning: "according to value." Used to describe real estate taxes based on the value of the property. (*Since the value of my land went up, my AD VALORUM taxes for last year were considerably higher than the year before.*)

ADVERSE POSSESSION   The right of a person to possess, live upon, and get title to a piece of land, even though he or she has no legal reason to claim that land nor is its legal owner. This type of possession is accomplished by living on the land, actually, continuously, hostilely, visibly, distinctly, and notoriously for a minimum length of time (set by each individual state), and not being ordered off by the rightful owners. (*My mother now owns land through ADVERSE POSSESSION, since she has openly lived on it for thirty years, and the owners never asked her to leave.*)

★AFFIDAVIT   A written statement sworn and given before a notary public or a government official or an officer who has the authority to administer oaths. (*I signed an AFFIDAVIT telling of my precise whereabouts last Saturday evening.*)

AFFIRM   A statement which says that the person affirming something is positively telling the truth.

★AGENCY   A contractual arrangement whereby one person (the principal) authorizes another person (the agent) to do things on his or her behalf. (*I have hired Hal's Real Estate AGENCY to sell my home.*)

★AGENT   One who is delegated to perform duties for another. (*Jerry has been my insurance AGENT for many years.*)

★AGREEMENT FOR SALE (DEED)   A written contract between buyer and seller in which the buyer agrees to buy, and the seller agrees to sell, upon certain terms and conditions, and upon a mutually agreed upon price. (*I just signed an AGREEMENT FOR SALE on my house.*)

AIR RIGHTS   The right of using the air space above the land which is owned. Technically, when you buy a piece of land, you own from the center of the earth through the boundaries of that land out into far space. However, in actuality, the government controls the air space of its domains. (*When my neighbor's store sign overhung onto my property, I asked him to set it back because he was violating my AIR RIGHTS.*)

★ALLOTMENT   A share or portion of something. Certain lands come with certain government allotments for crops, timber, tobacco, etc. (*The tobacco ALLOTMENT on my farm pretty well pays the mortgage.*)

★AMENITY   Anything which makes a piece of property more desirable, such as location on water, the view, nice trees, good pasture, etc.

★AMORTIZATION   The gradual paying off of a debt in small installment payments. (*The AMORTIZATION of my loan is over a 20-year period, but I can pay it off anytime I wish, without penalty.*)

ANNEX   An action of joining to something. It is usually used by a town or city in acquiring land which adjoins its boundaries. (*My property is not in the city yet, but I think they are going to ANNEX it next year.*)

*ANNUAL   Occurring yearly.

ANNUITY   A specific amount of money which is part of a specific series of payments for a specific period of time. *(Her social security check is an ANNUITY.)*

APEX   The highest point of something.

APPORTIONMENT OF TAXES   See *Adjustments*.

*APPRAISAL   The process of estimating the value of a piece of property by an expert. *(The APPRAISAL of our property was $10,000. We had hoped for $15,000.)*

APPRAISED VALUE   The probable value of a piece of property given by an expert. *(The APPRAISED VALUE of that building is $100,000.)*

*APPRECIATION   The increase in value of a piece of property. *(The APPRECIATION of that 50-acre tract could be as high as 5 to 10 percent per year.)*

*APPURTENANCE   Anything that is not actually part of the composition of the property, but is permanently attached to it, such as a building, a barn, a fence, a right-of-way, or anything you legally purchased when you purchased the property.

ASSESSED VALUE (VALUATION)   The value placed on a piece of property by a public officer for the purpose of taxation. *(The ASSESSED VALUE of my farm is $40,000, but I could easily sell it for $100,000.)*

ASSESSMENT   A charge made against land by a government body, usually for the purpose of paying for specific things, such as sidewalks, sewer systems, water systems, or other public works items which will serve the particular property involved. *(My sewer ASSESSMENT last year was more than I had expected it to be.)*

ASSESSOR   A government official responsible for figuring the values of properties on which assessments are made. *(I called the ASSESSOR about my property, but he would not reduce my assessment.)*

*ASSIGN   To turn over to, to give. *(He will ASSIGN the mortgage to you when you assume the seller's loan.)*

ASSIGNED MORTGAGE   A mortgage which has been transferred or sold by one lender to another.

ASSIGNEE   The one to whom a contract or agreement is assigned. *(I am the ASSIGNEE on my mother's mortgage.)*

*ASSIGNMENT   The way that a contract or agreement is transferred from one person to another.

ASSIGNOR   The one who assigns a contract or agreement from one person to another. *(As the ASSIGNOR of the contract, I assure you everything is in order.)*

*ASSIGNS   Those people who receive the benefit of an assignment. *(Since you are the ASSIGNS on this contract, I will be dealing with you in the future.)*

*ASSUMED MORTGAGE   An existing mortgage on a piece of property held by the seller which is taken over by the buyer.

*ATTACHMENT   A legal way in which some property can be held by the court after a judgment has been granted in a legal action.

*ATTEST   To swear that something is true and genuine. *(I can ATTEST that he has the right to sell his property.)*

AVULSION   This is the opposite of accretion. It means the loss of land or soil due to the changing water or stream bed. *(I have lost almost a half acre this year due to AVULSION.)*

BENCHMARK   See *Monument*.

BENEFICIARY   The person who receives the benefits of something, such as a will. *(I am my father's only BENEFICIARY.)*

BEQUEATH   Means to leave something to someone in a will. *("I BEQUEATH to my wife and children all my earthly possessions.")*

BEQUEST   Any item or items left to someone in a will. (*The money that the church received was from a BEQUEST.*)

BETTERMENT   Any improvement to property, such as sewers, sidewalks, streets, etc.

BILL OF SALE   A written document passing ownership of *something other than land* from seller to buyer. (*When I bought that used refrigerator, I received a BILL OF SALE.*)

BINDER   An agreement to cover the down payment for the purchase of real estate as evidence of good faith on the part of the purchaser. (*I made a BINDER on that piece of property down by the river today.*)

BLANKET MORTGAGE   A single mortgage covering more than one piece of property. (*I got a BLANKET MORTGAGE on all three of those pieces of property that I bought the other day.*)

BLOCK   A portion, usually a square, of city or town property containing streets.

*BONA FIDE   Latin for "in good faith." (*My broker brought me a BONA FIDE offer on my house.*)

*BOND   A sworn promise to perform, backed up by something of value. Usually it is bought from a bonding company which guarantees a specific payment, should the promise be broken. (*Some states require brokers to take out a BOND before they can sell property in that state.*)

*BORROWER   One who receives funds from a lender or lending institution and is responsible for repaying the loan.

BOUNDARY   The dividing line between two pieces of property. (*That fence is the BOUNDARY between my property and Bill's.*)

BRANCH   A small stream.

BREACH   To break a legal contract.

*BROKER   A person who is employed by another to perform certain duties. (*See Real Estate Broker.*)

BROOK   A small stream.

*BUILDING CODE   Regulations set down by governing bodies, usually towns, cities, or counties, concerning the way that buildings and other structures are to be constructed. (*I know my house is sound, since it was built according to a very strict BUILDING CODE.*)

*BUILDING LINE   A line of setback from the edge of the property past which no buildings or structures can extend in any direction. (See *Setback.*) (*My BUILDING LINE is twenty-five feet from the edge of my property.*)

CALENDAR YEAR   The twelve-month period beginning January 1 and ending December 31.

*CAVEAT EMPTOR   Latin for "let the buyer beware," meaning that the buyer should be very cautious and totally aware of everything he or she can find out about the property before buying. The actual entire quote is *caveat emptor qui ignorare non debuit quod jus alienum emit,* meaning "let the buyer beware who ought not to be ignorant that he is purchasing the rights of another."

*CERTIFIED CHECK   An official check drawn on a bank or a savings and loan institution, guaranteeing payment for the amount shown. (*If a deed is to be issued, usually payment has to be made by CERTIFIED CHECK.*)

CHAIN   See *Measurements.*

CHAIN OF TITLE   See *Abstract of Title.*

CHATTEL MORTGAGE   A mortgage using personal property, something other than land, as collateral. (*Since it was a CHATTEL MORTGAGE, I gave them my jewelry as collateral.*)

CHATTELS   Any living or non-living objects, including any goods other than real property.

CLEAR TITLE   See *Fee Simple.*

CLOSED MORTGAGE   A mortgage that, if paid off earlier than it is supposed to be, would require a penalty to be paid by the borrower.

*CLOSING STATEMENT   A written accounting of all monies figured at the consummation of the sale (closing) between buyer and seller. It outlines all charges and payments associated with the sale. (*I can keep my CLOSING STATEMENT as a record of the transaction.*)

*COLLATERAL   Any item(s) of value that a borrower pledges as security for a loan. (*My home and lot are COLLATERAL for the mortgage to the bank.*)

COLLUSION   When two or more people get together to steal from, or try to cheat, a third person. (*The two fellows who tried to cheat me out of the land were found guilty of COLLUSION.*)

*COMMISSION   The money paid to an agent or broker for performing certain duties. (*My broker really earned his COMMISSION in selling our dilapidated home.*)

*COMMITMENT   A pledge or a contract from a financial institution or other lender pledging to issue a mortgage or finance a home for a buyer. (*I got the bank to give me a COMMITMENT on that house on Beeker Street.*)

CONDEMNATION   The taking of private land for public use. (*In order to get the necessary land for the new roadway, the government had to resort to CONDEMNATION.*)

CONDOMINIUM   A privately owned apartment, town house, or cluster house, which is part of a larger development made up of many units.

*CONSIDERATION   Anything of value in a contractual arrangement to purchase something. (*Many contracts simply state: "For $1.00 and other valuable CONSIDERATION this transaction will be completed. . . ."*)

CONTIGUOUS   See *Adjoining.*

*CONTRACT   An agreement between two or more parties to do or avoid doing certain things in return for some sort of legal consideration. The result of the contract is that ownership passes from seller to buyer. (*We're scheduled to sign the CONTRACT of sale tomorrow.*)

CONVEY   To transfer title from one party to another.

CONVEYANCE   The document or means by which title of land is transferred. (*That land contract is a CONVEYANCE of land.*)

COOPERATIVE   An apartment, town house, or building, which is owned by a non-profit, cooperative corporation; each participant owns stock in that corporation.

COURTESY   The husband's rights in his wife's estate at the time of her death. It is to the husband what dower right is to the wife.

*COVENANT   A deeded agreement between two or more parties whereby the parties promise to do or avoid doing certain things.

CUBIC FOOT   See *Measurements.*

*CULVERT   A man-made ditch usually used to run off the excess water from land.

CULVERT PIPE   A pipe usually under a road or embankment which permits the water travelling through a culvert to continue under the ground.

DECEDENT   A dead person.

DEDICATION   The action of a private individual giving land to the government for the purpose of public use, and accepted by an official of the government for that use.

*DEED   A written document, properly signed and sworn before a notary or officer of the government, which transfers land from seller to buyer. (*When I paid off the land, they gave me a DEED to the property.*)

*DEED OF TRUST   A document containing a note which gives temporary title of a piece of property to a trustee until the note is repaid. (*When I bought the property, I had to sign a DEED OF TRUST for the money I borrowed.*)

DEFAULT   The failure to perform the promises and obligations stated in a contract. (*Because I didn't meet the obligations of the mortgage, the court found me in DE-FAULT.*)

DEFEASANCE   A document which cancels out the legal action of a deed or an estate. (*We finally got the land parcel through DEFEASANCE.*)

DEFENDANT   The person charged in a criminal action or sued in a civil action. (*I was the DEFENDANT in the trial when I was caught speeding and had to go to court.*)

*DELINQUENT   Not paying something when it is due.

DELIVERY   The change of possession of something from one person to another. (*We take DELIVERY of the deed on June 1.*)

DEMAND NOTE   A loan or note which states that the holder or lender may demand payment back at a specified time.

DEPARTMENT OF HOUSING AND URBAN DEVELOPMENT   See *H.U.D.*

*DEPOSIT   A small amount of money given at the time of the signing of the agreement to show good faith on the part of the buyer.

*DEPRECIATION   A loss in value of something due to wear and tear, becoming outdated, or simply damaged due to time. (*Since my business car is becoming older and less valuable, I can deduct the DEPRECIATION from taxes.*)

DESCENT   The passing of property from a dead person to his heirs.

DEVISE   A gift of land or real property through a will.

DEVISEE   The person who receives the devise.

DEVISOR   The one who gives the devise.

*DIRECT REDUCTION MORTGAGE   A mortgage in which the principal or the amount of money that was originally loaned is lessened by making equal payments. (*I have a typical home mortgage. It is a DIRECT REDUCTION MORTGAGE, because I make equal payments every month.*)

*DISBURSEMENTS   Payments, usually paid out on a specifically agreed upon basis. (*Once the loan goes through, DISBURSEMENTS will have to be made to all the persons to whom money is owed.*)

*DISCOUNT   An amount of money sometimes deducted from a loan at the time the loan is made, either as a substitute for part of the interest or in addition to the interest. For example: If you are going to borrow $10,000 from a certain lender, and that lender is giving you a discounted loan, then he might deduct $200, $300, $400, or whatever is decided, from the $10,000 he is lending you, so you don't actually get the whole $10,000. It is a type of additional charge that most lenders make in order to cover the costs of processing the loan.

*DISPOSSESS   To legally evict or throw a tenant or former owner off property which you own, or to which you have just been given title.

DISTRESS SALE   See *Forced Sale.*

*DOCUMENTARY STAMPS   A state tax which is charged when recording a mortgage note or deed. In a transfer of property, federal documentary stamps are required.

*DOMICILE   The place where a person has his or her permanent residence.

DONOR   The maker of a gift; the person who gives something to another.

DOWER RIGHTS   The rights that a widow has in her husband's estate at his death. (See *Courtesy.*)

*DOWN PAYMENT   The amount paid at the time of the purchase. It is not included in the total amount of the mortgage. (*The DOWN PAYMENT on my $60,000 home was $20,000, leaving me with a $40,000 mortgage.*)

DUE DATE   The day or date on which something, such as a monthly payment, is due to be paid. *(The DUE DATE on the monthly payments is the tenth of every month.)*

DUPLEX   A single house which is occupied by two separate families; it has two distinct separate entrances and one common wall or floor.

*DURESS   Pressure or some type of force or coercion to make you perform some act, possibly against your will.

DWELLING UNIT   A place where someone lives.

*EARNEST MONEY   A small amount of money paid at the time of the initial offer-to-purchase to show good faith on the part of the buyer. *(I put down $1,000 as EARNEST MONEY on my land purchase.)*

*EASEMENT   The right to use someone else's land in a certain manner specified by the landowner (to put in a water line, to put in an access road, etc.).

EJECTION   Similar to eviction except that ejection occurs when there is no agreement or contract between tenant or trespassing party and land owner.

*EMINENT DOMAIN   The right of a government to take or confiscate private property for public use. (See *Condemnation.*) *(He didn't want to sell his farm, but the government needed it for a State Park, so they paid him the appraised value and took it through EMINENT DOMAIN.)*

*ENCROACHMENT   The unlawful use of someone else's land. *(He built a fence on my neighbor's property; he was therefore guilty of ENCROACHMENT.)*

*ENCUMBRANCE   Anything which legally decreases the value of something else. *(The lien placed by the as-yet-unpaid brick mason is an ENCUMBRANCE on that new house.)*

*EQUITY   The value that one owns in a piece of property over and above the part that is under mortgage. It is the amount of paid principal. *(After paying on my land for four years, I had over $4,000 EQUITY in it.)*

EQUITY OF REDEMPTION   The right of the borrower to get his or her property back before the lender forecloses on the property, even though he or she stopped making payments and was found in default.

*EROSION   The wearing away of property or land through natural processes of water and wind.

EROSION CONTROL   The measures taken to prevent erosion from occurring or to minimize its effects.

ESCHEAT   Property going back to the government because there are no heirs or beneficiaries who are in line to inherit it. *(A smart person should never die intestate or heirless, or his or her estate will ESCHEAT to the state.)*

*ESCROW   Usually the deposit money held by the broker until the papers of the sale are concluded, when it is turned over to the seller. Escrow is also a deed which is held by a third person until the fullfillment of a contract concerning that deed. *(The broker deposited our earnest money in his ESCROW account until the deal was closed.*

*ESTATE   The total amount of property which a person owns in his or her life. *(Not being very rich, I have a rather small ESTATE.)*

ESTOPPEL CERTIFICATE   A document showing the amount owed by the borrower on a specific date.

*ET AUX   Latin for "and wife." *(Make the deed out to John Jones, ET AUX.)*

*EVICTION   The forcible throwing out of a tenant by a landlord. *(If you miss another month's rent, you will be subject to EVICTION.)*

*EXCLUSIVE AGENCY   A contractual arrangement with a broker, making that broker the only agent who can sell the property for you. However, you, as the owner, retain the right to sell the property on your own if you wish.

*EXCLUSIVE RIGHT TO SELL   If these words appear in your contract, then no one, not even you, as the owner, can sell the property for the duration of the listing contract unless the listing broker gets a commission. These terms hold even after the listing contract has expired if the buyer was brought by the broker during the term of the contract.

*EXECUTE   To do something or to make something happen, usually in a legal sense.

EXECUTION   A legal document issued by a court forcing the sale of property in order to satisfy a debt.

EXECUTOR   A man named in a will to fulfill the terms of a will by administering its various directives. *(I was named the EXECUTOR of my father's will.)*

EXECUTRIX   The female form of the word executor.

*F.H.A.   The FEDERAL HOUSING ADMINISTRATION, a branch of the government which insures private loans. The F.H.A. itself does not lend money nor construct houses, but rather guarantees the lender a specific percentage of the note should the borrower fail to pay.

FAIR MARKET PRICE   See *Market Price.*

FAIR MARKET VALUE   See *Market Value.*

FEDERAL HOUSING ADMINISTRATION   See *F.H.A.*

*FEE   Payment or a reward given for professional services. *(A broker's FEE is based on a percentage of the sale.)*

FEE ABSOLUTE   See *Fee Simple.*

*FEE SIMPLE   States that a person owns a piece of property totally and completely, with everything on it, and with no reservations. In other words, the owner owns the timber rights, the water rights, air rights, the right to will the property or to sell the property as he or she feels fit. *(Please make sure that the deed reflects that I have FEE SIMPLE ownership to that property.)*

FIDUCIARY (TRUST)   One who acts for another as a trustee or in a capacity of trust. A broker has a fiduciary relationship with his or her clients, as does an attorney.

*FIRST MORTGAGE   The mortgage that is the first lien on any property; should the property have to be foreclosed upon, that mortgage would have to be first paid off before anybody else (a lender holding a second or third mortgage) was paid anything.

*FISCAL YEAR   Any 12-month period within which a company or person, for accounting and tax purposes, operates or does business. A fiscal year may or may not differ from the calendar year.

FIXTURES   Any item attached to land, such as a building, a fence, a bridge, etc.

FORCED SALE   A sale of property which is forced by either the courts or an individual. It is a sale under duress (also called distress sale). (See *Duress.*)

*FORECLOSURE   A legal procedure through which a person's property, which had been put up as security for a loan (collateral), is sold to pay back the lender and satisfy the terms of the loan.

FORESHORE   The land between the high-water mark and the low-water mark on the shoreline of a body of water.

FORFEITURE   The loss of something of value, money or something else, as a penalty for failure to perform an act described in a contract. *(He failed to act on his promise, and he lost his deposit by FORFEITURE.)*

FRAUD   An intentional lie or falsehood resulting in the loss of something valuable or the loss of the rights of another party. *(He was convicted of FRAUD and he is now in jail.)*

FREEHOLD   An interest in real estate in fee simple, meaning absolute ownership of real estate.

FREEHOLDER   One who owns real estate.

FRONT FOOT   Refers to the measurement of property by the foot on the frontage of a road or body of water.

*FRONTAGE   Refers to property which adjoins another at its front. *(Although his land is in excess of 10 acres, he has only a 500-foot FRONTAGE on the state highway.)*

*GENERAL WARRANTY   An agreement in a deed by which the seller or grantor agrees to protect the buyer or grantee against all comers, technically "against the world." In other words, if you buy a piece of land and you have a general warranty in the deed, then if a brickmason comes back to you because he hasn't been paid for laying some bricks, the seller would have to pay him because he guaranteed through the warranty that it was a clear deed. *(Please make certain that I get a GENERAL WARRANTY deed to that unfinished house and property.)*

GOOD AND MARKETABLE TITLE   See *Marketable Title.*

GRANT   A legal term indicating the giving of something by someone to another. *(By signing this deed, I GRANT you all the lands indicated in the deed.)*

GRANTEE   The person or persons to whom title in a certain piece of real estate is given.

GRANTOR   The person who gives title of real estate to someone else.

GUARANTEE   A promise to perform certain acts or a pledge that something is in a certain state or condition; should the pledge turn out to be untrue, the party will make good in some manner.

*H.U.D.   The DEPARTMENT OF HOUSING AND URBAN DEVELOPMENT of the federal government; the watchdog over any land transactions which fall within their jurisdiction. This is the government agency you turn to if you have complaints concerning the purchase of land.

*HECTARE   See *Measurements.*

*HEIR   The legal descendant of a person who will, upon the death of that person, receive something of value. *(He is one of my five children, so he is not my only HEIR.)*

HEREDITAMENTS   A legal term which encompasses all property, be it tangible or intangible, such as a right-of-way. *(The property I bought was deeded with all HEREDITAMENTS, including mineral rights.)*

*HOMESTEAD   The home and property occupied by a person as a permanent residence. A homestead carries certain legal rights, such as protection against being attached under specific conditions or taken for sale by creditors (again under certain conditions).

HOMESTEAD EXEMPTION   An exemption given in some parts of the country against certain taxes or a reduction of taxes given on a permanent home. *(My HOMESTEAD EXEMPTION saved me over $200 on my tax bill.)*

*HUNDRED-YEAR FLOOD PLAIN   Refers to any land which, by government projection, might flood in the next 100 to 200 years. 50-year and 25-year projections also exist, but the hundred-year flood plain is most commonly used.

*IMPROVED LAND   Land on which or to which something has been done in order to make it better than its natural state, e.g., putting a building on it, building a fence on it, building a road on it, clearing it.

INCOMPETENT   A person who is not able to manage his or her own affairs.

INHERITANCE   Something left or given, upon the death of a person, to the heirs.

*INSTALLMENT CONTRACT   An agreement to pay for a certain piece of personal property over a specified time; usually it calls for payment of both principal and interest and also for the seizure of the property in the event of default or non-payment. A real-property installment contract is called a Deed of Trust or Trust Deed. *(I bought my home on an INSTALLMENT CONTRACT calling for monthly payments over the next 30 years.)*

INSTRUMENT   A legal document which sets down in writing the rights of the parties in the agreement.

*INTEREST   The fee or the money paid for using someone else's money.

INTEREST RATE   The portion or percent of monies which is paid as interest on a loan. Example: If you take out a simple interest loan of $1,000 at 15 percent interest for a period of one year, the interest will be $150. You will then be required to pay back the $1,000 plus the $150 interest, or a total of $1,150.

INTESTATE   A person who dies leaving either no will or a will that is not legal. In such a case, the distribution of his estate is decided by a court. (See *Testate*.)

*IRREVOCABLE   Cannot be taken back or revoked, cannot be changed, cannot be altered in any way.

JEOPARDY   Peril or danger.

*JUDGMENT   A ruling by a court which says one individual owes something to another individual and specifies how much is owed. (*He wouldn't pay me the money he owed me, so I had to go to court and get a JUDGMENT against him.*)

LACHES   The delay on the part of a person on speaking out on something he has rights to. For example, if someone owes you a large sum of money and you do nothing about collecting it for many, many years, you will be guilty of laches. Because of that, the person may be able to get away with never paying you back at all.

*LAND CONTRACT   An agreement for the purchase of land by which the deed does not pass from seller to buyer until after the full amount of the payment is made. (*I bought my lot through a LAND CONTRACT so I won't get my deed until the last payment is made.*)

LANDLORD   A person who rents or leases land to another.

*LEASE   A contract or agreement wherein a person can occupy the property of another person under specific terms, usually involving the payment of rent. (*Our Hunting Club does not own that 100-acre tract, we simply LEASE it to hunt on.*)

*LEGAL DESCRIPTION   A description or the summation of the boundaries of a piece of property which is recognized by law as being enough to identify and locate the property positively. (*Under some conditions, a street address can be considered a LEGAL DESCRIPTION.*)

LESSEE   A person who is leasing or renting property.

LESSOR   The person who leases or rents property to someone else.

LICENSE   The privilege or right given by the state or a body of authority which permits someone to perform certain acts within the jurisdiction of that state.

*LIEN   A legal right or hold on a piece of property, preventing the owner from selling it or disposing of it in any way until the cause of the lien (such as monies that are owed, taxes that are owed, mortgages or judgments) is paid.

LIFE ESTATE   The ownership or use of property only for the life of the user.

LINK   See *Measurements*.

LIS PENDENS   A Latin term stating that some sort of action is pending on a particular piece of property. This kind of document should turn up during a title search, and would put the prospective buyer on notice that some sort of legal action could affect this land, should he or she purchase it.

*LISTING   An employment contract between a principal and his or her agent. In the case of real estate, the seller hires a real-estate broker to represent the seller as an agent in order to sell the seller's property. In some cases a buyer may employ a broker to look after the buyer's interest.

LITTORAL   Something that belongs to the shore at the edge of the sea or a lake. (See *Riparian Rights*.)

LITIGATION   The act of carrying on a lawsuit. In other words, if you sue someone, you are in litigation.

*LOAN   The renting out or the letting out of money with the understanding that the borrower will repay it, with or without interest, within a specified period of time.

*Lot A portion, piece, or parcel of land as it is noted in the public records. A lot technically may be any size of land; however, it usually refers to a smaller piece, such as a quarter, a half, an acre, or even several acres. Once the size gets past two-and-one-half or five acres, the land is usually referred to as a parcel or tract.

Lot Line The boundary line between the lot and something else.

Mandatory Something that must be done.

Market Price The highest price the seller can expect to get for his property, as well as the highest price that the buyer would have to pay in order to purchase the property. *(If a house is worth somewhere between $60,000 and $70,000, the MARKET PRICE might be around $68,000-$70,000.)*

Market Value The lowest price which a seller is likely to accept and the highest price a buyer would be willing to pay without compulsion. *(If a house is worth somewhere between $60,000 and $70,000, the MARKET VALUE might be around $60,000-$62,000.)*

Marketable Title A title which a Court of Equity decrees to be free of defects or encumbrances and must be acceptable to the purchaser, even though the purchaser does not necessarily agree with the court.

*Maturity The final payoff date of a mortgage; it is that day on which the mortgage will be paid in full.

*Meanders The directions, the turns, and the course which a stream or river or any flowing body of water takes. In the description of boundaries, you may run across statements that say the boundary line runs with the meanders of a certain stream. This simply means that the boundary runs down the middle of the stream, no matter what the actual course of that stream. Should the stream change its course by natural means, you would either gain or lose land. (See *Avulsion* and *Accretion.*)

Mechanic's Lien A lien or a legal hold on a property placed by a workman in order to be paid for work performed upon the land. If you buy land with a mechanic's lien or any lien against it, you may become responsible for the payment of that lien, and you won't be able to sell the property or mortgage it without removing it.

*Measurements

Acre: 43,560 square feet, or 4,840 square yards, or 160 square rods.

Ares: $\frac{1}{100}$ of a hectare, or 100 square metres, or 119.6 square yards.

Chain: approximately 66 feet, or 4 rods.

Cord (Firewood): 128 cubic feet.

Cubic Foot: Imagine a box that is 12 inches wide, 12 inches high, and 12 inches deep—it will be 1 cubic foot.

Cubic Yard: 3 cubic feet wide, 3 high, and 3 deep; 27 cubic feet.

Front Foot: One lineal foot in length along the frontage of a lot. A lot that is 100 feet wide at the front where the street is, would have 100 front feet.

Furlong: 220 yards.

Hectare: 2.471 acres, or 100 ares.

League (Land): 3 statute miles.

Link: The hundredth part of a chain, so that in a chain, which is 66 feet, there are 100 links. A link is also 7.92 inches.

Metre: 39.37 inches, or just a little over a yard.

Mil: $\frac{1}{1000}$ of an inch.

Perch: See *Rod.*

Point: 0.013837 inches, or $\frac{1}{72}$ of an inch.

Pole: A rod.

Rod: 16½ feet, or 5.5 yards, or 25 links.

Section: 640 acres, or 1 square mile.

Square Mile: 640 acres.

Statute Mile: 5,280 feet, or 1,760 yards, or 80 chains, or 320 rods.

Township: 36 square miles, encompassing 23,040 acres.

Yard: 36 inches, 3 feet, or 0.9144 metres.

⋆METES AND BOUNDS   A description of a piece of land on which the boundaries are generally uneven and defined by directions and distances. In many cases, old deeds are done in this manner, using natural items, such as trees, stumps, or streams, as corners or boundary marks.

MILL   Not to be confused with the mil found under Measurements, a mill is equal to ¹⁄₁₀th of one cent, and is mostly used in taxation.

MILLAGE RATE   The use of the mill in figuring taxes on property. For example, a tax rate of 84 mills would mean that the property is being taxed at $8.40 per $1,000 of evaluation, or, if you own property worth $10,000 the tax bill would be $84.

⋆MINERAL RIGHTS   The rights of ownership of minerals, whether gaseous, liquid, and solid, which are on or under a piece of property. (*My father sold the farm, but he kept the MINERAL RIGHTS so that we will still be able to get the money from the oil well.*)

MINOR   A person not of legal age, be that 18 or 21, depending on how it is specified by law.

MISREPRESENTATION   To tell a lie; it is a falsehood or a misstatement of fact.

MONUMENT   Any visible object used to mark the line or corner of property. Surveyors usually use iron pipes, while government monuments, especially those designating large sections of land, are usually made of concrete and stamped on the top.

MORATORIUM   A period of time during which the borrower is permitted to delay doing whatever the contract calls for. (*Since you have a payment due and you can not make it, go to the bank and ask them for a delay. They may or may not grant you a MORATORIUM, in order to give you enough time to make the payment.*)

⋆MORTGAGE   A written document, properly filled out and signed, that puts a lien against the property for which it is signed, and outlines a schedule and method of payment to pay back the monies which have been loaned. (*If it weren't for the liberal terms of the bank MORTGAGE, I would not have been able to buy my home.*)

MORTGAGEE   The person who borrows the money and is obligated to repay the debt or the mortgage.

MORTGAGOR   The lender of the money and the holder of the mortgage.

MULTIPLE LISTING   A method/service that cooperating real-estate brokers have of exchanging their listings in order to be able to sell more houses faster by giving them wider exposure to potential buyers. In the sale of property, it is usually to your benefit to deal with a broker who is a member of Multiple Listing so that your property will get the widest possible advertising.

⋆NATURAL BOUNDARIES   Nature's boundaries, rather than man's, such as a river, a stream, a ridge line.

⋆NET LISTING   A contract with a broker denoting an amount of money below which the buyer will not accept a sale. The broker must add his or her commission to the net amount called for in the contract.

⋆NOTARY PUBLIC   A Notary Public is an officer of the state and county in which he or she lives. These public witnesses are authorized to witness anything on behalf of the world.

⋆NOTARIZE   Notarization is the act by which a Notary Public witnesses a document. To be legal, a notarization must include the notary's name, country of residence and expiration date of his or her commission, along with the date of the witnessing.

⋆NOTE   A document signed by one person making an absolute commitment to promise to pay someone else a certain amount of money. For example: A mortgage contains a note. The note is the piece of paper or the document in which the borrower of the money promises to repay the money to the lender.

OATH   A promise or statement saying that something is absolutely true.

OBSOLESCENT   Outdated (obsolete), usually because of physical or economic reasons.

OCCUPANCY   Occupancy is the condition of residing, living, or being in something.

*OCCUPANT   A person who occupies or lives in something.

*OFFER   In real estate, a written statement offering to purchase a piece of property for a specified amount. It must always be accompanied by money or a deposit of some sort.

ONE-HUNDRED-YEAR FLOOD PLAIN   See *Hundred-Year Flood Plain.*

OPEN-END MORTGAGE   A mortgage which you can expand by borrowing more money than the original amount without going through all new paperwork.

*OPEN LISTING   A listing with a broker, either spoken or written, which is not exclusive, meaning that any broker can try to sell the property. This type of listing is little more than a formal spelling out of the selling price and terms.

OPEN MORTGAGE   An open mortgage is one which can be paid off at any time without a penalty.

*OPTION   The right a buyer buys from a seller to purchase a piece of property for a certain price within a specified period of time. Example: A piece of property is priced at $20,000, but you are not certain that you want to buy it; you want to wait 30 days, but you don't want to lose the property to another buyer and you don't want to risk the price going up. What you do is offer an option on the property (say, $400 for 30 days). At the end of 30 days, if you don't buy the property, you lose your $400. However, if you do buy, then the seller must sell it to you at the $20,000 price and deduct the $400 from that price.

ORAL CONTRACT   A contract which is not written, but is simply spoken between parties.

ORIGINATION FEE   A charge, usually by a bank, based on a certain percentage of the mortgage or loan. This fee is sometimes called points. (See *Discount.*)

OUTHOUSE   A properly designed outside toilet which substitutes for putting in a septic system. In many states, it must be made flyproof, and is also known as a "privy."

PARCEL OF LAND   Land recorded as a single piece, usually owned by one person. It is considered to be a unit of land, and is more or less a very large lot.

PARISH   "County" in the state of Louisiana.

PARTITION   A division of the ownership of land or personal property formerly held in common. *(When the partnership was dissolved, the land was PARTITIONED among the partners.)*

*PARTY TO BE CHARGED   The person or party who must sign or execute an agreement or document. *(If you are the person selling a piece of land and giving a deed to that land, the buyer [the person to whom you are selling it] does not sign the deed. Only you need to sign the deed because you are the only PARTY TO BE CHARGED.)*

PARTY LAW OR PARTY FENCE   A division between two pieces of land or two buildings, half of which is owned by one person and half by the other.

PATENT   There are two meanings to a patent: (1) An exclusive right given by a government for a specified period to an inventor or his heirs or assigns, protecting something that he or she invented, be it an article or a process. (2) A document or instrument by which the government gives land that it owns to private persons.

PATENTED LAND   Land formerly owned by a government and granted or sold or given to a private owner by voluntary methods.

*PAYOFF   When a lender gives you the payoff figure, the lender is telling you how much principal and interest is left owing on your debt as of a certain date. The payoff is that amount of money which you have to pay in order to totally pay back the money you borrowed. *(My banker told me that the PAYOFF on my mortgage is $30,065.41.)*

PENHOOKER   In some parts of the country this slang term is used to describe an unlicensed real estate broker or any person who sells real estate illegally without a license.

*PERCOLATION TEST   An analysis of soil or earth which tells whether or not and how fast that particular soil will absorb water. It is sometimes necessary in order to be able to know whether a septic-tank system will function properly in a particular soil.

PERSONALITY   See *Personal Property.*

*PERSONAL PROPERTY   In law, only land and things attached to it are called real estate or real property. Personal property is everything else that a person owns, even though it may be many times more valuable than the real property. (See *Chattels.*)

PLAINTIFF   A person in a suit bringing the charge; it is the complaining party.

*PLAT   A recorded map of a specific piece of real estate that includes a very specific legal description and survey.

PLAT BOOK   The book or public record in which plats are kept.

PLOTTAGE   The size, shape and location of a piece of property in relation to other like pieces of property. It also refers to the gathering together of several parcels of land into a single unit.

POINTS   See *Origination Fee.*

POLE   See *Measurements.*

POSTPONEMENT OF LIEN   See *Subordination.*

*POWER OF ATTORNEY   A written document signed by the owner of any property, giving another person the power to act on behalf of the owner under certain conditions. *(Since Grandmother is getting old and feeble, she has given me POWER OF ATTORNEY to handle her affairs.)*

PREPAYMENT CLAUSE   Part of a mortgage which gives the borrower the privilege of paying off the mortgage at any time.

*PREPAYMENT PENALTY   A penalty or fee which a borrower may have to pay in order to pay off a mortgage earlier than the due date.

PREPAYMENT PRIVILEGE   See *Prepayment Clause.*

PRICE   The money necessary to buy something.

PRIMA FACIE   Latin for evidence at "first hand," meaning the obvious evidence or the obvious facts about something. *(The police had PRIMA FACIE evidence that he burned Mr. Miller's barn.)*

*PRINCIPAL   Principal has two meanings. (1) The employer of an agent or of someone who acts on the employer's behalf. (See *Agency.*) (2) The basic amount of money borrowed. In repaying a mortgage, the payments are made up of interest ("rent" paid on the money) and principal.

PRIVY   See *Outhouse.*

PROBATE   A procedure by which the courts process, or are involved in processing, someone's will.

PROBATE COURT   See *Surrogate's Court.*

*PROPERTY   Property refers to some tangible thing, either real (which refers to land) or personal (which refers to everything else).

PROPERTY LINE   The boundary or border between two pieces of land.

PRO RATA OR PRORATE   Latin, meaning a "fixed proportion" of something.

PROSPECTUS   A presentation or booklet which tells about some piece of property, and is usually put out by companies selling land in lots. It may or may not include the financial statement of the company and other information which may be of interest to the buyer.

QUIET ENJOYMENT   The right of an owner or person who legally owns a piece of property to enjoy it without interference from anyone.

QUIET TITLE SUIT   A lawsuit in a court which, if won, removes any defects or clouds from the title. For example, if you buy a piece of property having a lien against it, and you go to court to try the case to remove that lien, this action is called a Quiet Title Suit.

QUIT CLAIM DEED   A deed to a piece of property giving over title and interest to the new owner by way of release, while in no way guaranteeing that the title is valid or that other owners of that property may not buy it. The owner is simply giving up all rights to, and "quitting," literally, any claim to the property through a quit claim deed.

REAL ESTATE   Land and anything attached to the land.

REAL ESTATE BOARD   A group of appointed individuals who regulate the real estate industry in each state.

*REAL ESTATE BROKER   A person who has the right by law and license to sell land and represent both the buyer and seller. The broker has the right to hire salesmen and other brokers and to complete the sale by working up the closing statement.

REAL ESTATE SALESPERSON   A person licensed to sell real estate through the office and under the license and supervision of a broker.

REAL ESTATE TAX   A tax placed on property and paid by the property owner, usually to the city or county in which the property is located.

REAL PROPERTY   See *Real Estate*.

*REALTOR   A copyrighted and coined word referring to a member of a local real-estate board which is affiliated with the National Association of Real Estate Boards. Brokers are not automatically realtors.

*RECORDING   The act of placing on public record by entering into a book of public records various items and instruments, such as deeds or contracts, which have to do with the sale of property.

REDEMPTION   The right of the borrower or mortgagee to redeem or buy back property even after the property's payment due date has passed and after the expiration date. He or she may do this by paying the debt and usually a penalty.

REFINANCING   Reborrowing money to pay an existing debt. For example: You originally borrowed $10,000, and you still owe $8,000, but you need $15,000. If you refinance your loan, you will have to borrow $23,000. $23,000 will pay off the $8,000 of your original debt and leave you a balance of $15,000.

REFUND   To repay or to restore money; repayment of money.

*RELEASE   To give up something, or quit the claim, or drop the interest in an item, such as land.

*RELEASE CLAUSE   A clause in a mortgage which permits the buyer or borrower to release title to certain portions of a larger piece of land, based on the reduction of the amount of principal which has been paid.

REMAINDER   What is left after an estate is dissolved or terminated. For example, if your father has a life estate and can live on a certain piece of land for life, and if when he dies if there is a provision in that estate that you are to inherit five acres of land out of the original life estate, that five acres becomes the remainder.

REMAINDER MAN   The person who receives the remainder of an estate.

RENT   The money or compensation paid for the use of some property, such as land, a building, or an apartment.

REPLACEMENT VALUE   The cost of rebuilding or replacing an item which has been destroyed, lost, or stolen.

REPLEVIN   The return or recovery of goods or items which were wrongfully taken by somebody.

*RESIDENCE   The house or home or place in which a person has his actual dwelling and in which he is actually living.

*RESTRICTIONS   Limitations put on a piece of property, usually in the deed, by the previous owner.

*RESTRICTIVE COVENANTS   See *Restrictions*.

REVALUATION   The reappraisal of property by the taxing body.

REVERSION   The action in which property returns to the former owner after a certain item, e.g., a life estate, is terminated. For example: You have five acres of land and a house in which you have permitted your uncle a life estate. When he dies, that property again reverts to you as the owner.

REVERSIONARY CLAUSE   A clause or a statement in a deed which states that if certain restrictions or stipulations are not met, the property will revert to the seller, the person who imposed the restrictions. (*If I don't keep the pastures in good order, the REVER-SIONARY CLAUSE in my deed gives the seller the right to take back the land.*)

REVOCATION   The act of terminating or recalling power of authority and ending a certain condition.

RIGHT OF REDEMPTION   See *Redemption*.

RIGHT OF SURVIVORSHIP   The right of the surviving joint owner (either husband or wife) to get the interest or the ownership in whatever property is involved.

*RIGHT-OF-WAY   The right or authority to pass over someone else's land according to the nature of the right-of-way. (See *Easement*.)

RILL   A small brook or stream.

RIPARIAN RIGHTS   The rights to use the banks of a river, stream or waterway. (*My RIPARIAN RIGHTS run 200 feet out into the lake.*)

RISK   An insurance term which refers to the losses from which an insured person or company will be protected by a contract of insurance.

*RURAL PROPERTY   Property in the countryside as opposed to property in the city.

SALE ON THE COURTHOUSE STEPS   The forced sale of property by order of the court. Such a sale is usually held on the courthouse steps, in the form of an auction.

SALES AGREEMENT (SALES CONTRACT)   A document, a contract, in writing, between a buyer and a seller to buy property according to various terms.

*SATISFACTION   The settlement of a problem or payment that was due.

SATISFACTION OF MORTGAGE   When the mortgage has been completely paid off, it is termed to have been satisfied.

SATISFACTION PIECE   A document or instrument which states that the lender acknowledges receipt of payment in full for a debt. (*When I paid off my mortgage, I received a SATISFACTION PIECE.*)

*SECOND MORTGAGE   A mortgage on property which is second to a first mortgage. Example: If you own a $50,000 home and you have a $20,000 mortgage on it, you can go to a second mortgage lender and get money, say another $5,000, and take a second mortgage on the house. That would mean that you would owe a total of $25,000; $20,000 in the first mortgage and $5,000 in the second. In some cases, third mortgages are available if there is enough value in the property.

SECTION A unit of land laid out by a government survey, usually containing 640 acres; approximately one mile square (See *Measurements.*)

⋆SECURITY The money (or something of value) given or pledged toward the fulfillment of a promise or contract. (*Since I want to buy the land but don't have enough for the down payment, I'll have to use some stock as SECURITY in order to borrow the money.*)

SECURITY DEED See *Deed of Trust.*

SERVICE CHARGE A fee charged for the performance of some sort of service. In the case of a bank or a lender, it can mean points, or a percentage of the loan, as a fee for servicing that loan and handling it.

SETBACK The distance from the boundary of the property within which no construction can be done. (See *Building line.*)

SEVERALTY OWNERSHIP Despite its name, this is ownership by *one* person only, another way of saying sole ownership, because it is "severed" from others.

SHORE The land at the edge of a body of water.

SIMPLE LISTING See *Open Listing.*

SKY LEASE The rent or lease of the airspace above land. For example, if you have a piece of property on a street and someone wishes to hang a sign, part of which is going to protrude over your property, you would have the right to charge him a fee for using the airspace which that sign will take up.

SPECIAL ASSESSMENT An assessment or tax made against a piece of property, with the money going for improvement or improvements that the property paying the assessment is most likely to benefit from. For example, if there are no sidewalks in front of your house and the city decides to put in sidewalks, they will probably assess you for some or all of the value of the cost of the sidewalks.

⋆SPECIAL WARRANTY DEED A deed in which the grantor or seller limits his own liabilities to anyone making any claims through him. In other words, the seller is taking responsibility for any clouds or any indebtedness that he has anything to do with, but if there is anything on the property that possibly was there before the seller owned it, then no responsibility is taken for that.

SPECIFIC PERFORMANCE An act by a Court of Equity which forces the defendant to carry out the terms of an agreement or contract. For example: You buy something that does not do what it's supposed to do, and the seller won't give you satisfaction by fixing or replacing it. If you take him to court, and the court tells him that he must do what the contract says, they are ordering "specific performance."

⋆STATUTE A law of the land, state or federal.

⋆STATUTE OF FRAUDS A law requiring that all contracts for the sale of real estate be written, contain the necessary terms of the agreement, and be signed by the party to be charged. If all of the above are not part of the contract, and the contract is not in writing, it is a fraudulent sale of land.

⋆SUBDIVISION A piece or tract of land which has been divided, according to certain specific guidelines, into lots, and is suitable for some type of living or building sites. Usually, there are codes called subdivision ordinances, zoning ordinances, or building codes which govern the construction of any structures which go into a subdivision. If you are going to buy in a subdivision, check with the county in which the subdivision exists to see if there is a subdivision ordinance. If so, check to see if the subdivision is governed by that ordinance.

SUBLET To re-rent or lease something which you are renting or leasing from somebody else. For example: You rent an apartment and sign a one-year lease. After two months you are promoted to a job in another city. Instead of breaking your lease, losing your deposit, and hurting your credit rating, you rent the apartment to someone else for the balance of your lease obligation; this is called subletting.

SUBORDINATION CLAUSE   A clause in a contract which permits a new mortgage to supersede an earlier mortgage. For example: An uncle lends you money to buy a house, and takes a mortgage on the house as security. Five years later you need to borrow some more money. Your uncle can't lend it to you, so you go to your bank. The bank will not loan you any money unless it is the primary mortgagor, so you get your uncle to agree to subordinate, meaning to convert his first mortgage to a second and allow the bank to hold a first mortgage. This action is done through a subordination clause.

SUBPOENA   A legal document which commands a person to appear in court and sets a penalty for failure to appear. (Latin for "under pain of" penalty.)

SUBROGATION   The substitution of another person or party in place of the lender or creditor. For example: If you buy a piece of land in a subdivision, the subdivider, or the developer, can then sell your contract (if you buy by contract) to a bank or other third party. In doing so, the developer is subrogating the contract. You still owe the same amount of money at the same interest rate on the same terms to that bank, but no longer to the developer. This way the developer can get his principal (money) out much faster than by waiting for you to pay off the loan.

SUE   The action in which you take someone to court on a complaint and ask the court to resolve the problem.

SUNDAY CONTRACT   Certain states have very strict laws concerning activities on Sunday. In some states it is (or used to be) illegal to sign a contract on Sundays. Check the laws in your state. If such a law is in effect, no contract signed or dated on a Sunday will be legal.

SURETY   A person or company who or which guarantees the performance of another. In other words, the Federal Housing Authority (FHA) is a surety in that it guarantees the loan (up to a certain percentage) that you make with a bank through the FHA.

SURRENDER   The voiding or cancellation of a lease or a contract when both parties agree and consent to that cancellation.

SURROGATE'S COURT (PROBATE COURT)   A legal court of law which has powers with regard to the settling of estates and the proving of wills.

*SURVEY   A process by which land is measured and divided. Those measurements and divisions are printed on special papers in order to produce a type of map of the land. The word survey also applies to the piece of paper or map which shows the boundaries and measurements of the land.

SURVIVORS   See *Right of Survivorship*.

TAX DEED   A deed, usually given by a government agency, in cases where property has been purchased at a public sale, usually for non-payment of taxes.

TAX RATE   See *Millage*.

TAX ROLL (TAX LIST)   A listing of the parties or persons eligible to be taxed for certain things. For example, if you own property, then you are on the tax roll of the county in which you own that property, and you must pay taxes to that county and/or city.

TENANCY AT WILL   A person may occupy lands or buildings at the will of the owner, and if the owner changes his mind at any time, then the person has to leave.

*TENANCY BY THE ENTIRETY   A condition that exists *only* between husband and wife, each having equal rights of possession of a piece of property, which is jointly owned with survivorship.

*TENANCY IN COMMON   The ownership of property or buildings by two or more persons, none of whom are married to one another, without the right of survivorship, meaning that it is an undivided share type of ownership. For example: If four people buy a piece of property, should one of them die, the other three do not get the decedent's share. That share goes into the decedent's estate, and then to the heirs.

★TENANT   One who takes possession or is given possession of property for a certain period of time under certain conditions. If you rent an apartment or if you lease a piece of land, you are a tenant.

TENANT AT SUFFERANCE   A person or party who comes into possession of property by lawful means, but keeps it without a title.

TENANTS BY THE ENTIRETY   The husband and wife spoken of in the term Tenancy by the Entirety.

★TERM   The period of time of a mortgage or note. In other words, if you buy a home, and you take a 20-year mortgage, the term of that mortgage is 20 years.

TERM MORTGAGE   See *Term*.

★TESTATE   A person who dies leaving a valid and legal, properly signed will. (The opposite of intestate.)

TIME IS OF THE ESSENCE   A very specific term which means that the time specified in the contract is a very important part of that contract, and is a material element of the transaction or sale. If the sale is not completed or if certain things are not done within the time specified, the contract will not be accepted.

★TITLE   Legal evidence of ownership and legal possession of property.

TITLE BY ADVERSE POSSESSION   Ownership of land due to the occupation of that land, rather than due to holding title. This rarely happens, but in certain cases, if you live on a piece of land long enough, you might be able to get title by adverse possession. Don't count on it, though.

★TITLE INSURANCE   An insurance policy which protects the buyer from any loss because of defects in the deed. For example: You buy a piece of land, have a title search made, and buy title insurance. Initially, nothing wrong turns up, but later it turns out that there is a mechanic's lien of $5,000 against the property. Since a title search has been made, and you bought the title insurance, the insurance company would be obligated to pay the mechanic's lien or pay for the legal action to eliminate the lien from the property.

★TITLE SEARCH   A search which is usually conducted by an attorney on behalf of the buyer or the lending institution. It is done for the purpose of finding out if the title is clear. A title search in itself is not a guarantee of clear title. It is best to get title insurance. Many attorneys are covered themselves, however, and do guarantee title through an insurance company. In other words, the attorney will, for an additional fee, give you a letter stating that if there is anything wrong with the title, he or she is responsible. They have an insurance company that protects them.

★TOPOGRAPHIC MAP   A map or chart showing elevations, as well as other features, such as rivers, streams, roads, and some buildings. The elevations are shown by squiggly lines which are spaced at specific intervals and periodically show the elevation written in numbers.

★TOPOGRAPHY   The lay of the land; how flat or hilly it is.

TOWNSHIP   A legal description of land, encompassing 23,040 acres or 36 sections of land. (See *Measurements*.)

TRACT   Usually refers to a large area of land, much larger than a lot or plat.

TRANSFER FEE   A charge made at the time that one assumes another's mortgage. If, for example, you buy a piece of property that has a mortgage of $5,000 yet unpaid on it, and you assume that mortgage, you will probably have to pay a transfer fee to the bank or lending institution.

★TRESPASS   To enter illegally and traverse another's property without permission.

Trespass only occurs if the property is clearly marked as not permitting entry or is evidently or obviously someone else's property.

★TRUST   A legal entity through which someone, other than the owner, holds that owner's property, be it real or personal, on that owner's behalf, within the bounds of certain rules and restrictions. For example: If you have young children, you may want to place into your will a trust which would provide that in the event of your death, this trust would be maintained by an attorney, a court, or anyone you name as trustee, for the benefit of your children until they are adults.

TRUST DEED   See *Deed of Trust.*

★TRUSTEE (FIDUCIARY)   A person or a legal entity, such as a court, which holds property in trust for someone else.

UNDIVIDED INTEREST   See *Tenancy in Common.*

UNENCUMBERED PROPERTY   Property which is free and clear of any liens, easements, or encumbrances of any kind.

URBAN RENEWAL   Usually refers to the redevelopment of slum areas of a city, with or without government assistance.

USURY   A rate of interest on a loan which is higher than that permitted by law.

★V.A.   The Veterans Administration, an agency of the Federal Government, which insures and guarantees mortgage loans for servicemen and women. That is one of its many functions.

V.A. GUARANTEED LOAN   A loan or mortgage which is insured by the Veterans Administration.

VACATE   To leave the premises or abandon the land.

★VALID   Authorized by law or legally sufficient; binding and proper.

★VALUABLE CONSIDERATION   A legally proper amount of money on which a contract can be enforced.

VALUATION   See *Revaluation.*

VARIABLE INTEREST LOAN   A loan in which the interest charged may vary according to some specified method.

VENDEE   The purchaser of property.

VENDOR   The seller of property.

VERIFICATION   A statement sworn before an officer, duly qualified by law, stating that the contents of a document are true.

VETERANS ADMINISTRATION   See *V.A.*

VOID   Unenforceable, not effective, or cancelled.

VOLUNTARY CONVEYANCE   When a mortgagee cannot meet his payments and voluntarily gives the property over to the mortgagor (the party holding the mortgage).

WAIVER   The surrender of a claim or the giving up of a right or privilege.

★WARRANTY   A promise that something is true.

★WARRANTY DEED   A conveyance for land or property in which the seller or grantor guarantees the title to the buyer.

WATER RIGHTS   The rights to use water from someone else's property, usually tied in with a water easement, which permits a person to cross another's land to a source of water.

WILL   A legal document which states how a person's property is to be handled and divided after that person's death.

WRIT OF EXECUTION   A document that authorizes a sheriff or a proper officer of the court to carry out the court's decrees.

★ZONING ORDINANCE   A law, usually within cities or municipalities, which states the limitations regarding the use of particular property.

Appendix 2

FORMS YOU ARE LIKELY TO SEE

SPECIAL NOTE: The forms shown and discussed in this appendix are purely samples. The actual form you may be given could differ substantially in various ways, or may be almost completely different, depending on the type of land transaction and the part of the country in which you are buying land. Since a contract for the purchase of land must be in writing, remember this rule: *Never sign anything unless you know exactly what the document you are signing requires you to do, and what it requires all the other parties to do. If you're not certain, don't sign. Get some help and advice from someone who is qualified.*

There are a large variety of forms and legal documents which you will come across during the land-purchase procedure. Forms, such as deeds, mortgages, deeds of trust, closing statements, notes, etc., will usually be drawn up by attorneys and prepared for you by either attorneys and/or real-estate professionals. For that reason, such forms are not depicted in this appendix. If you are not thoroughly familiar with such forms, consult a professional. Policies, as well, vary from state to state. If you're not dealing with a registered subdivision, be certain to also get professional guidance.

The forms that are depicted in this appendix are among the most common forms you will see. They are the Land or Property Receipt Contract, two Deposit forms, a Real Estate Option form, and an Offer to Purchase (Contract). Most forms you will come across will originally have been drawn by an attorney hired by the developer or seller, and will most naturally carry all the provisions that are beneficial to that developer or seller. You have to make certain that those provisions are not against your best interests. There may be absolutely nothing detrimental or harmful to you in the manner that the contract or form is written, but be certain you fully understand all the provisions in the document you're signing.

Beware of information from well-meaning friends. Many times, persons who think they know the right answers can lead you far astray. Even when such persons give you evidently correct information, it may turn out to be wrong. For example, it may be correct in their (and your) home state, but wrong in the state in which you're buying land.

Always get help from a local (to where the land is) professional. An attorney's or accountant's fee may seem relatively high, but compared to the thousands of dollars you stand to lose in an improperly handled land transaction, it is usually money very well spent. Some normally free professional advice can come from a real estate broker, especially one who is a Realtor (since a Realtor is pledged to an especially high code of ethics). A broker who is not connected with the sale (as a representative of the seller) will usually be happy to advise you, if you allow her or him to officially represent you in the sale. As a cooperating broker, he or she will share in a percentage (usually 50 percent) of the selling broker's commission, so such advice will normally cost you nothing except the time it takes you to find and check out such a broker (usually through the chamber of commerce, a local bank, savings and loan, or Board of Realtors).

LAND CONTRACTS

(*also called Property Agreements, Property Receipt Contracts, and a variety of other names*) These documents are all legally drawn documents which specify the terms of a land sale, and describe what will happen when the principal amount is paid off to a seller or lender by a buyer. Take special note, *a land contract is a legal promise. It's not a legal conveyance, such as a deed, and it does not convey land.* It only *promises* to convey the land once you've made your final payment. This document is only an agreement between the buyer and the seller, and unless it's recorded at a courthouse, it gives you no guarantee that the seller will be able to fulfill the promises stipulated in that contract. By recording the contract, you publish it for the world. You legally say that you and the seller (or developer) have a contract. This legally prevents the seller or developer from mortgaging or otherwise encumbering the property you are buying. *For a contract to be recordable, it must be notarized at the time of signing.*

IMPORTANT SPECIFICS TO KNOW ABOUT PROPERTY RECEIPT (LAND) CONTRACTS

Don't simply glance over it. Read every word of both the printed parts and the parts filled in by the salesman. The omission of a word or fact can make a major difference. Be certain that the land is properly described. In other words, Contract No. 1 does not refer to a recording in a plat book. If it is not a recorded subdivision, the actual survey description of your lot should appear somewhere on the contract. Since counties usually require subdivisions to record their plats (for tax purposes), you'll usually not find surveys on property receipt contracts, but be certain to ask for proof of the recording. If you are dealing with a non-HUD registered subdivision, be certain to use your development questionnaire listed in Chapter 13.

When buying land from a HUD registered subdivision, be certain that the wording at the bottom of the contract specifies 7-day and/or 2-year cancellation provisions. In a contract for a non-registered subdivision (but one that must conform to HUD anti-fraud provisions) be certain there is mention of the 20-day correction of default and the 85 percent return of principal.

The following three sample contract forms will probably be similar (or at least will contain the same information) to ones you will be presented should you buy from a development.

FORM A is a sample contract of a subdivision which does not fall under any provision of HUD. Note that there is no reference to a recording (that is a danger point). Also note that there is disclosure of total interest at the bottom of the contract. (If this is not included in your contract, be sure to ask and get the answer in writing.) *Remember*, unless there is reference to another document somewhere in the contract, only those provisions stipulated and guaranteed by the contract will be enforceable against the developer.

FORM B is a typical contract of a development that has registered with HUD. You must receive a Property Report as stipulated in the bottom portion of this contract.

FORM C is a sample of a non-HUD registered subdivision but one which must have HUD's anti-fraud provisions. It refers to a specific recording at a courthouse, the 20-day notification provision, and the 85 percent return of principal provision.

A SAMPLE LAND CONTRACT OF A NON-HUD REGISTERED SUBDIVISION

PROPERTY RECEIPT CONTRACT

DATE _____ , 19 _____

Purchase Agreement between THE A.B.C.D. CORPORATION and

_____*(NAME)*_____

Address _____   County _____

_____   Phone _____

Section _____   Tract _____

of

SUNNY ACRES SUBDIVISION

Total purchase price $ *4995.⁰⁰* . Down payment $ *495.⁰⁰* . Balance $ *4500.⁰⁰* . To be paid in cash by _____ or in *180* monthly installments of $ *56.94* beginning *(DATE)* . We hereby acknowledge receipt of $ *495.⁰⁰* as cash payment to be applied on this purchase, plus $ *100⁰⁰* settlement costs for a total of $ *595.⁰⁰* . It is understood that this Purchase Agreement is binding when approved by an Officer of THE A.B.C.D. CORPORATION and is subject to restrictions and easements as recorded. Warranty Deed will be delivered when total purchase price is paid. Total interest over *15* years at *13* % APR is $ *5749.20*. There is no prepayment penalty.

THE A.B.C.D. CORPORATION STIPULATES THAT THE PROPERTY LISTED ABOVE IS NOT NOW ENCUMBERED NOR TO THE BEST OF ITS ABILITY WILL BECOME ENCUMBERED FOR THE TERM OF THIS AGREEMENT. NO RECREATIONAL FACILITIES ARE PLANNED OR PROMISED. ALL UTILITIES ARE THE RESPONSIBILITY OF THE BUYER.

THE A.B.C.D. CORPORATION
Approved for The Corporation

_____
PURCHASER

_____   _____
PURCHASER

_____
NOTARY PUBLIC

Form A

A SAMPLE LAND CONTRACT OF AN HUD REGISTERED SUBDIVISION

PROPERTY RECEIPT CONTRACT

DATE _____ , 19 _____

Purchase Agreement between THE A.B.C.D. CORPORATION and
_____(NAME)_____

Address _____   County _____
_____   Phone _____
Section _____   Tract _____
of
SUNNY ACRES SUBDIVISION

Total purchase price $ *4495.00* . Down payment $ *445.00* Balance
$ *4050.00* . To be paid in *180* monthly installments of $ *51.25*
beginning *(DATE)* . We hereby acknowledge receipt of $ *445.00* as cash
payment to be applied on this purchase. ($ *0* balance of down payment due
_____.) It is understood that this Purchase Agreement is binding when
approved by an Officer of THE A.B.C.D. CORPORATION and is subject to restrictions and easements as recorded. Warranty Deed will be delivered when total purchase
price is paid.

YOU HAVE THE OPTION TO VOID THIS CONTRACT OR AGREEMENT IF
YOU DID NOT RECEIVE A PROPERTY REPORT PREPARED PURSUANT TO
THE RULES AND REGULATIONS OF THE U.S. DEPARTMENT OF HOUSING AND URBAN DEVELOPMENT IN ADVANCE OF, OR AT THE TIME OF,
YOUR SIGNING THE CONTRACT OR AGREEMENT; AND YOU HAVE THE
RIGHT TO REVOKE THE CONTRACT OR AGREEMENT WITHIN 7 DAYS
AFTER SIGNING THE CONTRACT OR AGREEMENT. IF YOU DID NOT
RECEIVE THE PROPERTY REPORT BEFORE YOU SIGNED A CONTRACT
OR AGREEMENT, YOU MAY CANCEL THE CONTRACT OR AGREEMENT
AT ANY TIME WITHIN 2 YEARS AFTER THE DATE OF SIGNING.

THE A.B.C.D. CORPORATION
Approved for The Corporation   _____
PURCHASER

_____   _____
PURCHASER

_____
NOTARY PUBLIC

Form B

A SAMPLE LAND CONTRACT OF A NON-HUD REGISTERED SUBDIVISION
(However, one which must meet HUD's anti-fraud provisions)

PROPERTY RECEIPT CONTRACT

DATE _____, 19 _____

Purchase Agreement between THE A.B.C.D. CORPORATION and *(NAME)*

Address _____   County _____

_____   Phone _____

Section _____   Tract _____

of

SUNNY ACRES SUBDIVISION

As recorded at (county) Courthouse

Total purchase price $ *3995.00* . Down payment $ *395.00* . Balance *3600.00* . To be paid in *180* monthly installments of $ *45.56* beginning *(DATE)* . We hereby acknowledge receipt of $ *395.00* as cash payment to be applied on this purchase. ($ *0* balance of down payment due _____.) It is understood that this Purchase Agreement is binding when approved by an Officer of THE A.B.C.D. CORPORATION and is subject to restrictions and easements as recorded. Warranty Deed will be delivered when total purchase price is paid.

IF YOU DEFAULT OR BREACH THIS CONTRACT, THE A.B.C.D. CORPORATION WILL GRANT YOU A MINIMUM OF 20 DAYS FROM THE RECEIPT OF THE NOTICE TO CORRECT THE DEFAULT OR BREACH, AND IF YOU LOSE YOUR RIGHTS AND INTEREST IN THE ABOVE LISTED LOT BECAUSE OF A DEFAULT OR BREACH ON YOUR PART, WE SHALL REFUND TO YOU ALL PRINCIPAL OVER AND ABOVE 15% OF THAT WHICH YOU HAVE PAID US AFTER WE HAVE DEDUCTED ANY ACTUAL DAMAGES.

THE A.B.C.D. CORPORATION
Approved for The Corporation

_____
PURCHASER

_____   _____
                                    PURCHASER

_____
NOTARY PUBLIC

Form C

DEPOSIT FORMS

Some sellers of land try to use deposit forms as binding contracts. Be careful of the deposit form wording, especially if you make a deposit on a piece of land being sold directly to you by the owner. The owner is not required to set your deposit money aside in any special manner, and, depending upon the exact wording of the deposit form, you may be hard put to get this money back should the sale not go through. When you are dealing with a real-estate professional, you must still be careful of what you sign, but by law that individual must place your deposit money in a special escrow account (in which no non-escrow monies are placed), and must either return that money to you or apply it against the sale, depending upon whether the sale does or does not go through. Here are two sample deposit forms:

DEPOSIT FORM to be signed if you are *certain* of obtaining the financing you need:

Received from _____ *(NAME)* _____ (Buyer) $_____
deposit on real estate at *(LAND OF MY DREAMS, U.S.A.)*
_____ Price $*100,000.⁰⁰*
A properly drawn Contract to be signed within *20* _____ days and additional deposit to be made up to *20* ____% of the purchase price.
_____ 19 _____   _____ (Seller)

* * *

DEPOSIT FORM to be signed if you are *uncertain* of obtaining the financing you need:

Received from _____ *(NAME)* _____ (Buyer) $*1000.⁰⁰*
deposit on real estate at *(LAND OF MY DREAMS, U.S.A.)*
_____ Price $*125,000.⁰⁰*
Buyer is to get deposit back if unable to obtain a $*100,000.⁰⁰* mortgage at ____*15*_% for ____*10*____ yrs.
A properly drawn Contract to be signed within *30* _____ days and additional deposit to be made up to *25* ____% of the purchase price.
_____ 19 _____   _____ (Seller)

REAL ESTATE OPTION FORM

Through the Real Estate Option Form, you tie up the property for a specific length of time by paying a set amount of money to the seller. If, within that specified period of time, you decide to buy the land according to the provisions in the option agreement, your option money is usually applied against the price of the property. If you decide not to buy the property, you lose the money you paid for the option.

Be certain that a proper description of the property is shown on the option form (use the reverse side of the form if necessary), and be certain that all the terms are totally and absolutely specified in detail at the bottom of the form.

One of the most common mistakes made in optioning a piece of property is not giving yourself enough time to accomplish the things you need to accomplish in order to make a proper decision regarding the ultimate purchase of the land. There is no set rule to go by, but in bargaining for the length of time, start with much more than you feel the seller will give you, and let him cut you back. In this manner, you will let him set the longest period of time he will permit you.

REAL ESTATE OPTION

_____ , 19 _____

The undersigned SELLER hereby acknowledges receipt from the undersigned BUYER of the sum of $ *500.⁰⁰* for the OPTION to purchase the real estate located at *(LAND OF MY DREAMS, U.S.A.)* _____

_____
for a sale price of $ *75,000.⁰⁰*. This option to bind the seller from this date until *(6 MOS. HENCE)* 19 _____ at noon. The said sum to be applied as part of the purchase price, if the buyer avails himself of this option and so notifies the seller in writing before the expiration of this option.

Should the buyer NOT so avail himself, the above sum shall become the property of the seller in payment for keeping said property off the market, and all parties shall be released from further obligation under this option.

Should the buyer avail himself of the right to purchase under this option, and so notify the seller, the above amount will be applied to the purchase price, and an additional deposit of $ *19,500.⁰⁰* will be made then. The sale will be under the terms of the agreement attached hereto as it is initialed by the parties.

The seller agrees to hold the amount herewith deposited IN ESCROW for the benefit of the buyer for the option period, and if the buyer shall notify him of his intention to complete the purchase, until the passing of papers, and should the seller be unable to perform in accordance with the agreement, all said amounts shall be returned to the buyer. This contract shall bind the parties, their heirs and legal representatives. (Insert other terms here.)

_____
_____
_____
_____

WITNESS
our hands and seals:

SELLER _____   SELLER'S SPOUSE _____
BUYER _____   BUYER'S SPOUSE _____
                                   BROKER _____

CONTRACT OR OFFER TO PURCHASE

This is a document that will spell out all of the details and specifics concerning your purchase of property. Standard forms are available and are used by most real estate professionals. This form reflects everything the seller is willing to do with regard to the sale, as well as everything the buyer must do in order to acquire the property. *IF IT'S NOT WRITTEN IN THIS AGREEMENT, IT LEGALLY DOESN'T EXIST, AND NEITHER THE BUYER NOR THE SELLER IS OBLIGATED TO ANY PROMISES OUTSIDE THOSE IN THE CONTRACT.*

Unless you thoroughly and completely understand all the aspects of the Contract or Offer to Purchase, *GET PROFESSIONAL ASSISTANCE* from an attorney or real estate professional.

The form I've shown is one commonly used and is relatively self-explanatory. Refer to the glossary if there are any words you don't fully understand.

CONTRACT OR OFFER TO PURCHASE

_____(NAME)_____, as Buyer, hereby agrees to purchase and _____(NAME)_____, as Seller, hereby agrees to sell and convey all of that plot, piece or parcel of land described below, together with all improvements located thereon and such personal property as is listed below (the real and personal property are collectively referred to as "the Property"), in accordance with the Standard Provisions ATTACHED HERETO and upon the following terms and conditions:

1. REAL PROPERTY: Located in the City of _____, County of _____, State of _____, being known as and more particularly described as:

Street Address _RT. 1, BOX 40_____
Legal Description _AS PER DEED RECORDED IN PLAT BOOK 450, PAGE 92_____

2. PERSONAL PROPERTY: _LAWN EQUIPMENT, PICNIC TABLE, OLD TRACTOR AND EQUIPMENT._

3. PURCHASE PRICE: The purchase price is $ _150,000.⁰⁰_____
and shall be paid as follows:

(a) $ _1,000.⁰⁰_, in earnest money paid by _CHECK_____ (cash; bank, certified, or personal check) with the delivery of this contract, to be held in escrow by _____, as agent, until the sale is closed, at which time it will be credited to Buyer, or until this agreement is otherwise terminated and it is disbursed in accordance with the Standard Provisions ATTACHED HERETO.

(b) $ _55,000.⁰⁰_, by assumption of the unpaid principal balance and all obligations of Seller on the existing loan secured by a deed of trust on the Property;

(c) $ _____ , by a promissory note secured by a purchase money deed of trust on the Property with interest prior to default at the rate of _____% per annum, payable by _____ payments of $ _____ commencing on _____ . Prepayment rights, if any, shall be _____;

(d) $ _94,000.⁰⁰_ , the balance of the purchase price in cash at closing;

4. CONDITIONS: (Mark N/A in each blank space of paragraph 4 (a) and 4 (b) that is not a condition to this contract)

(a) The Buyer must be able to obtain a firm commitment for a _SECOND_ _MORTGAGE_ _____ loan in the principal amount of $ _25,000.⁰⁰_ for a term of _5_ years, at an interest rate not to exceed _15_% prior to _CLOSING_. Buyer agrees to advise Seller immediately upon his receipt of such firm commitment and to use his best efforts to secure such commitment.

(b) Mortgage loan discount points not to exceed _____% of the loan shall be paid by _____ and loan closing costs shall be paid by _____ .

(c) There must be no restrictions, easement, zoning, or other governmental regulation that would prevent the reasonable use of the real property for _____ _____ purposes.

5. ASSESSMENTS: Seller warrants that there are no encumbrances or special assessments, either pending or confirmed, for sidewalk, paving, water, sewer or other improvements on or adjoining the Property, except as follows: _NONE_

(Insert "none" or the identification of any such assessments, if any; the agreement for payment or proration of any assessments indicated is to be set forth in paragraph 6 below.)

6. OTHER PROVISIONS AND CONDITIONS:

(a) All of the Standard Provisions ATTACHED HERETO are understood and shall apply to this instrument, except the following numbered Standard Provisions shall be deleted: _NONE_ .

(If none are to be deleted, state "none" in this blank.)

(If additional space is needed, use that at the end of this form.)

7. CLOSING: All parties agree to execute any and all documents and papers necessary in connection with closing and transfer of title on or before _(DATE)_ , at a place designated by _(ATTORNEY)_ . Deed is to be made to _(BUYER)_

8. POSSESSION: Possession shall be delivered _AT CLOSING_ _____ ; in the event that Buyer has agreed that possession is not delivered at closing, then Seller agrees to pay to Buyer the sum of $ _50_ per day to and including the date that possession is to be delivered as above set forth.

9. COUNTERPARTS: This Offer shall become a binding contract when signed by both Buyer and Seller and is executed in ___*FOUR*_____ _____ counterparts with an executed counterpart being retained by each party hereto.

Date of Offer _____   Date of Acceptance _____

_____ (SEAL)   _____ (SEAL)
Buyer   Seller (Owner)
_____ (SEAL)   _____ (SEAL)
Buyer   Seller (Owner.)

_____   _____
Agent/Firm   Agent/Firm

    I hereby acknowledge receipt of the earnest money herein set forth in accordance with the terms hereof.

_____   _____
Date   Agent/Firm
                                        By: _____

STANDARD PROVISIONS

    1. EARNEST MONEY: In the event this offer is not accepted, or in the event that any of the conditions hereto are not satisfied, or in the event of a breach of this contract by Seller, then the earnest money shall be returned to Buyer, but such return shall not effect any other remedies available to Buyer for such breach. In the event this offer is accepted and Buyer breaches this contract, then the earnest money shall be forfeited, but such forfeiture shall not affect any other remedies available to Seller for such breach.

    2. LOAN ASSUMED: In the event a loan is assumed as part of the payment of the purchase price, then all payments due from Seller thereon must be current at closing, and the principal balance assumed shall be computed as of the date of closing. The amounts shown for the assumption balance and cash at closing shall be adjusted as appropriate at closing to reflect the final computations. Unless Buyer has otherwise specifically agreed in writing, the existing loan must be assumable without acceleration of the amount secured or any change in the original terms of the note and deed of trust and without imposition of any charge, fee or cost to Buyer other than a reasonable transfer fee or similar charge not to exceed $100.00. The escrow account, if any, shall be purchased by Buyer.

    3. PROMISSORY NOTE AND DEED OF TRUST: In the event a promissory note secured by a deed of trust is given by Buyer to Seller as part of the payment of the purchase price, and the promissory note and deed of trust shall be in the form of and contain the provisions of the promissory note and deed of trust forms approved by the Bar Association.

    4. PRORATIONS AND ADJUSTMENTS: Unless otherwise provided, the following items shall be prorated and adjusted between the parties or paid at closing:
    (a) Ad valorem taxes on real property shall be prorated on a calendar-year basis to the date of closing.
    (b) Ad valorem taxes on personal property for the entire year shall be paid by Seller.

(c) All late listing penalties, if any, shall be paid by Seller.

(d) Rents, if any, for the Property shall be prorated to the date of closing.

(e) Buyer shall have the right to purchase Seller's fire insurance policy upon payment to Seller of the unearned premium therefor, if the policy is assignable.

(f) Accrued, but unpaid, interest and other charges to Seller, if any, shall be computed to the date of closing and paid by Seller; interest and other charges prepaid by Seller shall be credited to Seller at closing and paid by Buyer. (Other charges may include FHA mortgage insurance premiums, private mortgage insurance premiums and Homeowner's Association dues.)

5. FIRE OR OTHER CASUALTY: The risk of loss or damage by fire or other casualty prior to closing shall be upon the Seller.

6. CONDITIONS:

(a) The Property must be in substantially the same condition at closing as on the date of this offer, reasonable wear and tear excepted.

(b) All deeds of trust, liens and other charges against the Property, not assumed by Buyer, must be paid and cancelled by Seller prior to or at closing.

(c) Title must be delivered at closing by general warranty deed and must be fee simple marketable title, free of all encumbrances except ad valorem taxes for the current year (prorated to date of closing), utility easements and unviolated restrictive convenants that do not materially affect the value of the Property and such other encumbrances as may be assumed or specifically approved by Buyer. The subject Property must have legal access to a public right-of-way.

(d) If a portion of the purchase price for the Property is being paid by assumption of an existing loan and if the lender requires its approval for the assumption, then the approval of the lender, after diligent application therefor by Buyer, is a condition of this contract.

7. NEW LOAN: Buyer shall be responsible for all charges made to Buyer with respect to any new loan obtained by Buyer, and Seller shall have no obligation to pay any discount fee or other charge in connection therewith unless specifically set forth in this contract.

8. UTILITIES: Unless otherwise stated herein, the electrical, plumbing, heating and cooling systems, and built-in appliances, if any, shall be in good working order at closing. Buyer has the option to have the same inspected by a reputable inspector or contractor at Buyer's expense, but such inspections must be completed in sufficient time before closing so as to permit repairs, if any, to be completed by closing. If any repairs are necessary, Seller shall have the option of (a) completing them, (b) providing for their completion, or (c) refusing to complete them. If Seller elects not to complete the repairs, then Buyer shall have the option of (a) accepting the Property in its present condition, or (b) terminating the contract, in which case the earnest money shall be refunded. Closing shall constitute acceptance of the electrical, plumbing, heating and cooling systems and built-in appliances in their existing condition unless provision is otherwise made in writing pursuant to this paragraph. (RECOMMENDATION: Buyer should have any inspections made prior to incurring expenses for closing.)

9. TERMITES, ETC.: Unless otherwise stated herein, Seller shall provide at Seller's expense a statement showing the absence of termites, wood-destroying insects and organisms and structural damage therefrom in accordance with the regulations of

the (State) _____ Structural Pest Control Committee or, if new con struction, a new construction termite bond. All extermination required and repair o damage therefrom shall be paid for by Seller and completed prior to closing, unless otherwise agreed in writing by the parties.

10. LABOR OR MATERIAL: Seller shall furnish at closing an affidavit and indemnification agreement in form satisfactory to Buyer showing that all labor or mate rials, if any, furnished to the Property within 12 days prior to the date of closing have been paid and agreeing to indemnify Buyer against all loss from any cause or claim arising therefrom.

11. FUEL OIL: Buyer agrees to purchase from Seller the fuel oil, if any, situated in a tank on the premises for the prevailing rate per gallon with the cost of measure ment thereof, if any, being borne by Seller.

12. CLOSING EXPENSES: Seller shall pay for the preparation of a deed and fo the revenue stamps required by law. Buyer shall pay for recording the deed and fo preparation and recording of all instruments required to secure the balance of the purchase price unpaid at closing.

13. EVIDENCE OF TITLE: Seller agrees to exercise his efforts to deliver to Buyer as soon as reasonably possible after the acceptance of this offer, copies of all title information in possession of or available to Seller, including but not limited to: title insurance policies, attorney's opinions on title, surveys, covenants, deeds, notes and deeds of trust and easements relating to the real and personal property described above.

14. ASSIGNMENTS: This contract may not be assigned without the written agreement of all parties, but if the same is assigned by agreement, then the same shall be binding on the Assignee and his heirs.

15. PARTIES: This contract shall be binding and shall inure to the benefit of the parties and their heirs, successors and assigns. The Provisions herein contained with respect to promissory notes and mortgages or deeds of trust shall be binding upon and shall inure to the benefit of all parties to the same as well as subsequent owners of the Property and the said mortgages, notes and deeds of trust. As used herein, words in the singular include the plural and the masculine includes the feminine and neuter genders, as appropriate.

16. SURVIVAL: Any provisions herein contained which by its nature and effec if required to be observed, kept, or performed after the closing shall survive the closing and remain binding upon and for the benefit of the parties hereto until fully observed kept or performed.

17. ENTIRE AGREEMENT: Buyer acknowledges that he has inspected the above-described property. This contract contains the entire agreement of the parties and there are not representations, inducements, or other provisions other than those expressed in writing. All changes, additions or deletions hereto must be in writing and signed by all parties. Nothing herein contained shall alter any agreement between Realtor and the Seller as contained in any listing contract or other agreement between them.

Appendix 3

AGENCIES YOU ARE LIKELY TO NEED

There are a variety of local, state, and federal agencies which can provide a wealth of information, much of it free of charge, on almost any aspect of land and land buying. Since it is easy to simply write each agency and ask for their list of publications, I have listed in this Appendix the topics or areas that each agency covers, rather than listing available publications. The addresses listed in this appendix are main office or regional office addresses. In many cases, these agencies have local area offices. Those addresses are available from the agency.

CONSUMER PRODUCT INFORMATION

Consumer Product Information
Public Documents Distribution Center
Pueblo, CO 81009

Topics: A variety of consumer-oriented publications with regard to various aspects of land and land buying.

GOVERNMENT PRINTING OFFICE

Government Printing Office
Superintendent of Documents
Washington, DC 20402

Topics: Detailed maps concerning geography, air circulation, precipitation, snowfall, temperature, growing seasons, waterways, etc., are available for most states.

U.S. DEPARTMENT OF AGRICULTURE (USDA)

U.S. Department of Agriculture
Office of Information
Washington, DC 20250

Topics: Available information on irrigation, water supplies, snow surveys, conservation, controlling unwanted vegetation, ponds, raising fish, wells, soil, septic tank systems, sewage-disposal systems, prediction of rainfall, erosion laws, waterflow, wind

erosion, salt-water intrusion, soil percability, fireplaces and chimneys, building founda-
tions, various house systems (such as heating, cooling, and plumbing), drainage, recreation development, farming for profit, rural zoning, and land laws.

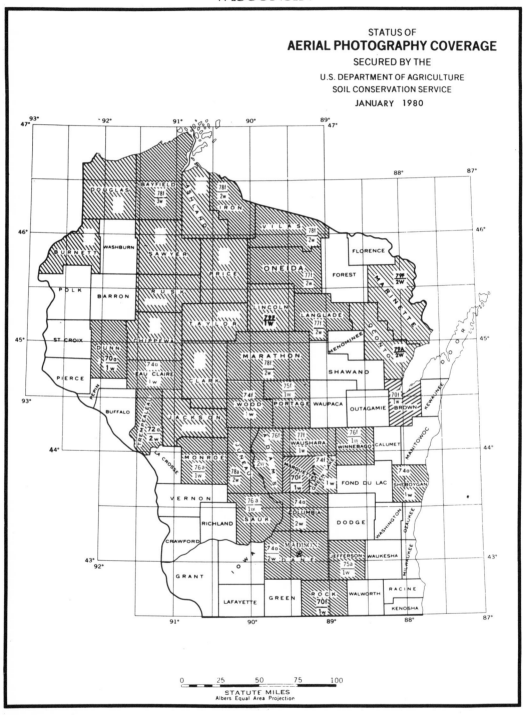

A U.S.D.A. aerial-photography-catalog map.

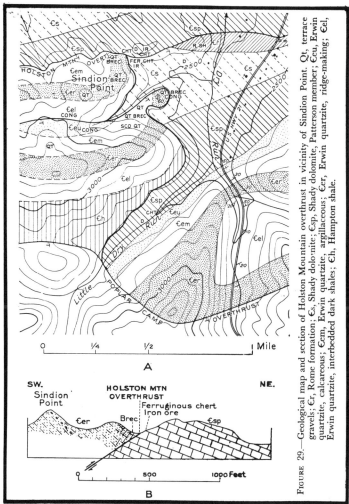

FIGURE 29.—Geological map and section of Holston Mountain overthrust in vicinity of Sindion Point. Qt, terrace gravels; €r, Rome formation; €s, Shady dolomite; €sp, Shady dolomite, Patterson member; €eu, Erwin quartzite, calcareous; €em, Erwin quartzite, argillaceous; €er, Erwin quartzite, ridge-making; €el, Erwin quartzite, interbedded dark shales; €h, Hampton shale.

A soil map. (From Bulletin #72, *Geology and Mineral Resources of the Gossan Lead District and Adjacent Areas in Virginia,* by Anna and George Stose.)

AGRICULTURAL STABILIZATION AND CONSERVATION SERVICE (ASCS)

Agricultural Stabilization
and Conservation Service
U.S. Department of Agriculture
Washington, DC 20250

Topics: Soil analyses, cooperative financing plans for soil improvement, aerial photographs, and general farm assistance.

FOREST SERVICE

Located in individual cities and
towns, usually at county seats.

Topics: Information on trees, ground covers, forest management, trees for profit, diseases of trees, and control of wood pests.

U.S. DEPARTMENT OF COMMERCE

SOIL CONSERVATION SERVICE (SCS)

> Soil Conservation Service
> U.S. Department of Agriculture
> Washington, DC 20250

Topics: Information on soils, erosion, ponds, and small dams.

WEATHER BUREAU

> U.S. Department of Commerce
> Weather Bureau, Climatological Section
> National Records Section
> Asheville, NC 28801

> U.S. Department of Commerce
> Environmental Science Services Administration
> Environmental Data Service
> Silver Spring, MD 20900

Topics: The local weather bureau in your area can provide most of the information you will need. If they can't, write to either of the above addresses.

U.S. DEPARTMENT OF HOUSING AND URBAN DEVELOPMENT (HUD)

OFFICE OF INTERSTATE LAND SALES REGISTRATION (OILSR)

> Office of Interstate
>   Land Sales Registration
> HUD Building
> 451 7th Street, S.W.
> Washington, DC 20410

Topics: Any and all information on the purchase of developed land, your rights as a buyer, and laws and regulations which protect you.

U.S. DEPARTMENT OF INTERIOR

BUREAU OF LAND MANAGEMENT (BLM)

> Bureau of Land Management
> U.S. Department of Interior
> Washington, DC 20245

Topics: Information on buying and using public lands, land reclamation, homesteading, and mining claims.

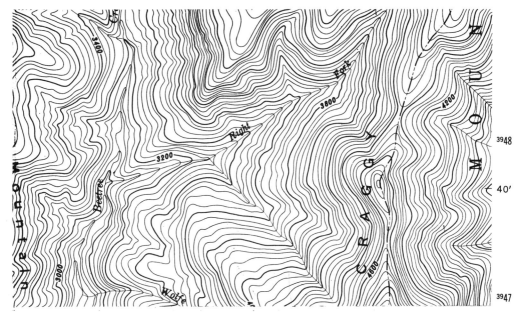

A topographic map shows the elevation of a piece of land. The numbers on the darker squiggly lines indicate feet of elevation at that point. The lighter lines show the spread by various elevations. (From the United States Department of the Interior Geological Survey, Tennessee Valley Authority Maps and Surveys Division)

U.S. GEOLOGICAL SURVEY

> U.S. Geological Survey
> U.S. Department of Interior
> Washington, DC 20242

Topics: Information on water, water cycles, lakes, water usage, rivers, surface and ground water, various water data activities, map and survey information, topographic maps, aerial photos, water and water use laws, minerals, and mineral deposits and extractions.

LOCAL ASSISTANCE

As mentioned earlier in the book, the following people can be of great assistance to you. They can usually be found through county or city courthouses.

County Administrator
County Building Inspector
County Engineer
County Health Inspector
County Planning Commissioner
County Road Commissioner
County School Superintendent
County Sheriff
County Surveyor
County Tax Assessor
Fire Chief

Appendix 4

TECHNICAL SOIL GLOSSARY

The list of terms that follows is representative of those used in soil and water conservation handbooks put out by various state agencies.

AASHO CLASSIFICATION (*soil engineering*)   The official classification of soil materials and soil aggregate mixtures for highway construction used by the American Association of State Highway Officials.

ACRE-FOOT   The volume of water that will cover one acre to a depth of one foot.

AGGRADATION   The process of building up a surface by deposition. This is a long-term or geologic trend in sedimentation.

ALLUVIAL   Pertaining to material that is transported and deposited by running water.

ALLUVIAL LAND   Areas of unconsolidated alluvium, generally stratified and varying widely in texture, recently deposited by streams, and subject to frequent flooding. A miscellaneous land type.

ALLUVIAL SOILS   An azonal great-soil group of soils, developed from transported and relatively recently deposited material (alluvium) characterized by a weak modification (or none) of the original material by soil-forming processes.

ALLUVIUM   A general term for all detrital material deposited or in transit by streams, including gravel, sand, silt, clay, and all variations and mixtures of these. Unless otherwise noted, alluvium is unconsolidated.

ANTI-SEEP COLLAR   A device constructed around a pipe or other conduit and placed through a dam, levee, or dike for the purpose of reducing seepage losses and piping failures.

ANTI-VERTEX DEVICE   A facility placed at the entrance to a pipe conduit structure such as a drop inlet spillway or hood inlet spillway to prevent air from entering the structure when the pipe is flowing full.

BEDROCK   The more or less solid rock in place either on or beneath the surface of the earth. It may be soft or hard and have a smooth or irregular surface.

BEDROCK, DEPTH   1. Shallow to bedrock. Less than 20 inches to solid bedrock. 2. Moderately deep to bedrock. 20 to 36 inches to solid bedrock. 3. Deep to bedrock. Three feet or more to solid bedrock.

BEDROCK, HARDNESS   1. Soft. Presents no excavation problems with modern equipment. 2. Medium. Presents some excavation problems with modern equipment. 3. Hard. Usually requires specialized techniques such as drilling and blasting for excavation.

BLINDING MATERIAL   Material placed on top of and around a closed drain to improve the flow of water to the drain and to prevent displacement during back-filling of the trench.

BLIND INLET   Inlet to a drain in which entrance of water is by percolation rather than open flow channels.

142

BORROW AREA A source of earth fill material used in the construction of embankments or other earth fill structures.

BOTTOM LANDS A term often used to define lowlands adjácent to streams.

CHANNEL A natural stream that conveys water; a ditch or channel excavated for the flow of water.

CHANNEL IMPROVEMENT The improvement of the flow characteristics of a channel by clearing, excavation, realignment, lining, or other means in order to increase its capacity. Sometimes used to connote channel stabilization.

CHANNEL STABILIZATION Erosion prevention and stabilization of velocity distribution in a channel using jetties, drops, revetments, vegetation, and other measures.

CHANNEL STORAGE Water temporarily stored in channels while en route to an outlet.

CONDUIT Any channel intended for the conveyance of water, whether open or closed.

CONSERVATION The protection, improvement, and use of natural resources according to principles that will assure their highest economic or social benefits.

CONSERVATION DISTRICT A public organization created under state-enabling law as a special-purpose district to develop and carry out a program of soil, water, and related resource conservation, use, and development within its boundaries, usually a subdivision of state government with a local governing body and always with limited authorities. Often called a soil conservation district or a soil and water conservation district.

CONTOUR 1. An imaginary line on the surface of the earth connecting points of the same elevation. 2. A line drawn on a map connecting points of the same elevation.

CONTOUR DITCH Irrigation ditch laid out approximately on the contour.

COVER CROP A close-growing crop grown primarily for the purpose of protecting and improving soil between periods of permanent vegetation.

CRADLE A device, usually concrete, used to support a pipe conduit or barrel.

CUT Portion of land surface or area from which earth has been removed or will be removed by excavation; the depth below original ground surface to excavated surface.

CUT-AND-FILL Process of earth moving by excavating part of an area and using the excavated material for adjacent embankments or fill areas.

CUTOFF TRENCH A long, narrow excavation constructed along the center line of a dam, dike, levee or embankment and filled with relatively impervious material intended to reduce seepage of water through porous strata.

DAM A barrier to confine or raise water for storage or diversion, to create a hydraulic head, to prevent gully erosion, or for retention of soil, rock, or other debris.

DEBRIS A term applied to the loose material arising from the disintegration of rocks and vegetative material; transportable by streams, ice, or floods.

DEBRIS DAM A barrier built across a stream channel to retain rock, sand, gravel, silt, or other material.

DEBRIS GUARD Screen or grate at the intake of a channel, drainage, or pump structure for the purpose of stopping debris.

DEGRADE The alteration of a channel caused by erosion and scour of the channel bottom.

DESIGN HIGHWATER The elevation of the water surface as determined by the flow conditions of the design floods.

DESIGN LIFE The period of time for which a facility is expected to perform its intended function.

DETENTION DAM A dam constructed for the purpose of temporary storage of streamflow or surface runoff and for releasing the stored water at controlled rates.

DIKE (*engineering*)   An embankment to confine or control water, especially one built along the banks of a river to prevent overflow of lowlands; a levee. (*geology*) A tabular body of igneous rock that cuts across the structure of adjacent rocks or cuts massive rocks.

DISCHARGE (*hydraulics*)   Rate of flow, specifically fluid flow; a volume of fluid passing a point per unit time, commonly expressed as cubic feet per second, million gallons per day, gallons per minute, or cubic meters per second.

DISCHARGE COEFFICIENT (*hydraulics*)   The ratio of actual rate of flow to the theoretical rate of flow through orifices, weirs, or other hydraulic structures.

DISCHARGE FORMULA (*hydraulics*)   A formula to calculate rate of flow of fluid in a conduit or through an opening. For steady flow discharge, $Q = AV$, wherein Q is rate of flow, A is cross-sectional area, and V is mean velocity. Common units are cubic feet per second, square feet, and feet per second, respectively. To calculate the mean velocity, V for uniform flow in pipes or open channels. (See *Manning's Formula*.)

DIVERSION   A channel with or without a supporting ridge on the lower side constructed across or at the bottom of a slope for the purpose of intercepting surface runoff. (See *Terrace*.)

DIVERSION DAM   A barrier built to divert part or all of the water from a stream into a different course.

DIVERSION TERRACE   Diversions, which differ from terraces in that they consist of individually designed channels across a hillside, may be used to protect bottomland from hillside runoff or may be needed above a terrace system for protection against runoff from an unterraced area. They may also divert water out of active gullies, protect farm building from runoff, reduce the number of waterways, and are sometimes used in connection with stripcropping, to shorten the length of slope so that the strips can effectively control erosion. (See *Terrace*.)

DRAIN   1. A buried pipe or other conduit (closed drain). 2. A ditch (open drain) for carrying off surplus surface water or groundwater. 3. To provide channels, such as open ditches or closed drains, so that excess water can be removed by surface flow or by internal flow. 4. To lose water (from the soil) by percolation.

DRAINAGE   1. The removal of excess surface water or groundwater from land by means of surface or subsurface drains. 2. Soil characteristics that affect natural drainage.

DRAINAGE, SOIL   As a natural condition of the soil, soil drainage refers to the frequency and duration of periods when the soil is free of saturation; for example, in well-drained soils the water is removed readily but not rapidly; in poorly drained soils the root zone is waterlogged for long periods unless artificially drained, and the roots of ordinary crop plants cannot get enough oxygen; in excessively drained soils the water is removed so completely that most crop plants suffer from lack of water. Strictly speaking, excessively drained soils are a result of excessive runoff due to steep slopes or low available waterholding capacity due to small amounts of silt and clay in the soil material. The following classes are used to express soil drainage:

Well drained   excess water drains away rapidly and no mottling occurs within 36 inches of the surface.

Moderately well drained   water is removed from the soil somewhat slowly, resulting in small but significant periods of wetness. Mottling occurs between 18 and 36 inches.

Somewhat poorly drained   water is removed from the soil slowly enough to keep it wet for significant periods but not all the time. Mottling occurs between 8 and 18 inches.

Poorly drained   water is removed so slowly that the soil is wet for a large part of the time. Mottling occurs between 0 and 8 inches.

Very poorly drained   water is removed so slowly that the water table remains at or near the surface for the greater part of the time. There may also be periods of surface ponding. The soil has a black-to-gray surface layer with mottles up to the surface.

DRAWNDOWN   Lowering of the water surface (in open channel flow), water table, or piezometric surface (in groundwater flow) resulting from a withdrawal of water.

DROP-INLET SPILLWAY   Overall structure in which the water drops through a vertical riser connected to a discharge conduit.

DROP SPILLWAY   Overall structure in which the water drops over a vertical wall onto an apron at a lower elevation.

DROP STRUCTURE   A structure for dropping water to a lower level and dissipating its surplus energy; a fall. A drop may be vertical or inclined. Syn.: drop.

EARTH DAM   Dam constructed of compacted soil materials.

EMBANKMENT   A man-made deposit of soil, rock or other material used to form an impoundment.

EMERGENCY SPILLWAY   A vegetated earth channel used to safely convey flood discharges in excess of the capacity of the principal spillway.

ENERGY DISSIPATOR   A device used to reduce the energy of flowing water.

ERODIBLE *(geology and soils)*   Susceptible to erosion.

EROSION   1. The wearing away of the land surface by running water, wind, ice, or other geological agents, including such processes as gravitational creep. 2. Detachment and movement of soil or rock fragments by water, wind, ice, or gravity. The following terms are used to describe different types of water erosion:

Accelerated erosion   Erosion much more rapid than normal, or geologic erosion, primarily as a result of the influence of the activities of man or, in some cases, of other animals or natural catastrophes that expose base surfaces, for example, fires.

Geological erosion   The normal or natural erosion caused by geological processes acting over long geologic periods and resulting in the wearing away of mountains, the building up of floodplains, coastal plains, etc. Syn.: natural erosion.

Gully erosion   The erosion process whereby water accumulates in narrow channels and, over short periods, removes the soil from this narrow area to considerable depths, ranging from 1 to 2 feet to as much as 75 to 100 feet.

Natural erosion   Wearing away of the earth's surface by water, ice, or other natural agents under natural environmental conditions of climate, vegetation, etc., undisturbed by man. Syn.: geological erosion.

Normal erosion   The gradual erosion of land used by man, which does not greatly exceed natural erosion. (See *Natural Erosion.*)

Rill erosion   An erosion process in which numerous small channels only several inches deep are formed; occurs mainly on recently disturbed and exposed soils. (See *Rill.*)

Sheet erosion   The removal of a fairly uniform layer of soil from the land surface by runoff water.

Splash erosion   The spattering of small soil particles caused by the impact of raindrops on wet soils. The loosened and spattered particles may or may not be subsequently removed by surface runoff.

EROSION CLASSES *(soil survey)*   A grouping of erosion conditions based on the degree of erosion or on characteristic patterns. Applied to accelerated erosion, not to normal, natural, or geological erosion. Four erosion classes are recognized for water erosion and three for wind erosion.

EROSIVE   Refers to wind or water having sufficient velocity to cause erosion. Not to be confused with erodible as a quality of soil.

ESCARPMENT   A steep face or a ridge of high land; the escarpment of a mountain range is generally on that side nearest the sea.

FLAT   Section of stream with current too slow to be classed as riffle and too shallow to be classed as a pool. Stream bottom usually composed of sand or fine materials, with coarse rubble, boulders, or bedrock occasionally evident.

FILTER BLANKET   A layer of sand and/or gravel designed to prevent the movement of fine-grained soils.

FILTER STRIP   A long, narrow vegetative planting used to retard or collect sediment for the protection of diversions, drainage basins, or other structures.

FLOOD   An overflow or inundation that comes from a river or other body of water and causes or threatens damage.

FLOOD CONTROL   Methods or facilities for reducing flood flows.

FLOOD CONTROL PROJECT   A structural system installed for protection of land and improvements from floods by the construction of dikes, river embankments, channels, or dams.

FLOODGATE   A gate placed in a channel or closed conduit to keep out floodwater or tidal backwater.

FLOOD PEAK   The highest value of the stage or discharge attained by a flood, thus, peak stage or peak discharge.

FLOODPLAIN   Nearly level land situated on either side of a channel which is subject to overflow flooding.

FLOOD ROUTING   Determining the changes in the rise and fall of floodwater as it proceeds downstream through a valley or reservoir.

FLOOD STAGE   The stage at which overflow of the natural banks of a stream begins to cause damage in the reach in which the elevation is measured.

FLOODWATER RETARDING STRUCTURE   A structure providing for temporary storage of floodwater and for its controlled release.

FLOODWAY   A channel, either natural, excavated, or bounded by dikes and levees, used to carry excessive flood flows to reduce flooding. Sometimes considered to be the transitional area between the active channel and the floodplain.

FLUME   A device constructed to convey water on steep grades lined with erosion-resistant materials.

FRAGIPAN   A natural subsurface horizon with high-bulk density relative to the solum above, seemingly cemented when dry but showing a moderate to weak brittleness when moist. The layer is low in organic matter, mottled, slowly or very slowly permeable to water, and usually shows occasional or frequent bleached cracks forming polygons. It may be found in profiles of either cultivated or virgin soils but not in calcareous material.

FREEBOARD   A vertical distance between the elevation of the design highwater and the top of the dam, levee, or diversion ridge.

GAGE OR GAUGE   Device for registering precipitation, water level, discharge, velocity, pressure, temperature, etc.

GAGING STATION   A selected section of a stream channel equipped with a gage, recorder, or other facilities for determining stream discharge.

GRADATION (*geology*)   The bringing of a surface or a stream bed to grade, by running water. As used in connection with sedimentation and fragmental products for engineering evaluation, gradation refers to the frequency distribution of the various-sized grains that constitute a sediment, soil, or other material.

GRADE   1. The slope of a road, channel, or natural ground. 2. The finished surface of, a canal bed, roadbed, top of embankment, or bottom of excavation; any surface prepared for the support of construction like paving or laying a conduit. 3. To finish the surface of a canal bed, roadbed, top of embankment, or bottom of excavation.

GRADED STREAM   A stream in which, over a period of years, the slope is delicately adjusted to provide, with available discharge and with prevailing channel characteristics, just the velocity required for transportation of the load (of sediment) supplied from the drainage basin.

The graded profile is a slope of transportation. It is a phenomenon in which the element of time has a restricted connotation. Works of man are limited to his experience and of design and construction.

GRADE STABILIZATION STRUCTURE   A structure for the purpose of stabilizing the grade of a gully or other watercourse, thereby preventing further head-cutting or lowering of the channel grade.

GRADIENT   Change of elevation, velocity, pressure, or other characteristics per unit length; slope.

GRADING   Any stripping, cutting, filling, stockpiling, or any combination, including the land in its cut and filled condition.

GRASS   A member of the botanical family *Gramineae*, characterized by bladelike leaves arranged on the culm or stem in two ranks.

GRASSED WATERWAY   A natural or constructed waterway, usually broad and shallow, covered with erosion-resistant grasses, used to conduct surface water from cropland.

GULLY   An incised channel or miniature valley cut by concentrated runoff but through which water commonly flows only during snow. A gully may be dendritic or branching or it may be linear, rather long, narrow, and of uniform width. The distinction between gully and rill is one of depth. A gully is sufficiently deep that it would not be obliterated by normal tillage operations, whereas a rill is of lesser depth and would be smoothed by use of ordinary tillage equipment. Syn. arroyo. (See *Erosion; Rill.*)

GULLY CONTROL PLANTINGS   The planting of forage, legume, or woody-plant seeds, seedlings, cuttings, or transplants in gullies to establish or re-establish a vegetative cover adequate to control runoff and erosion and incidentally produce useful products.

GULLY EROSION   See *Erosion.*

HABITAT   The environment in which the life needs of a plant or animal are supplied.

HEAD *(hydraulics)* 1. The height of water above any plane or reference. 2. The energy, either kinetic or potential, possessed by each unit weight of a liquid, expressed as the vertical height through which a unit weight would have to fall to release the average energy possessed. Used in various compound terms such as pressure head, velocity head, and lost head.

HEAD GATE   Water control structure; the gate at the entrance to a conduit.

HEAD LOSS   Energy loss due to friction, eddies, changes in velocity, or direction of flow.

HEADWATER   1. The source of a stream. 2. The water upstream from a structure or point on a stream.

HIGHWAY EROSION CONTROL   The prevention and control of erosion in ditches, at cross drains, and on fills and road banks within a highway right-of-way. Includes vegetative practices and structural practices.

HYDROGRAPH   A graph showing for a given point on a stream or for a given point in any drainage system the discharge, stage, velocity, or other property of water with respect to time.

IMPACT BASIN   A device used to dissipate the energy of flowing water. Generally constructed of concrete in the form of a partially depressed or partially submerged vessel and may utilize baffles to dissipate velocities.

IMPOUNDMENT   Generally, an artificial collection or storage of water, as a reservoir, pit, dugout, sump, etc.

INFILTRATION   The flow of a liquid *into* an area through pores or other openings, connoting flow into a soil in contradistinction to percolation, which connotes flow *through* a porous substance.

INLET *(hydraulics)* 1. A surface connection to a closed drain. 2. A structure at the diversion end of a conduit. 3. The upstream end of any structure through which water may flow.

INOCULANT   A peat carrier impregnated with bacteria which forms a symbiotic relationship enabling legumes to utilize atmospheric nitrogen. Most legumes require a specific bacterium.

INOCULATION   The process of introducing pure or mixed cultures or micro-organisms into natural or artificial cultural media.

INTAKE   1. The headworks of a conduit, the place of diversion. 2. Entry of water into soil. (See *Infiltration.*)

INTAKE RATE   The rate of entry of water into soil. (See *Infiltration.*)

INTENSITY   See *Rainfall Intensity.*

INTERCEPTION *(hydraulics)*   The process by which precipitation is caught and held by foliage, twigs, and branches of trees, shrubs, and other vegetation. Often used for "interception loss" or the amount of water evaporated from the precipitation intercepted.

INTERCEPTION CHANNEL   A channel excavated at the top of earth cuts, at the foot of slopes or at other critical places to intercept surface flow; a catch drain. Syn.: interception ditch.

INTERCEPTOR DRAIN   Surface or subsurface drain, or a combination of both, designed and installed to intercept flowing water.

INTERFLOW   That portion of rainfall that infiltrates into the soil and moves laterally through the upper soil horizons until intercepted by a stream channel or until it returns to the surface at some point downslope from its point of infiltration.

INTERMITTENT STREAM   A stream or portion of a stream that flows only in direct response to precipitation. It receives little or no water from springs and no long-continued supply from melting snow or other sources. It is dry for a large part of the year, ordinarily more than three months.

INTERNAL SOIL DRAINAGE   The downward movement of water through the soil profile. The rate of movement is determined by the texture, structure, and other characteristics of the soil profile and underlying layers and by the height of the water table, either permanent or perched. Relative terms for expressing internal drainage are: none, very slow, slow, medium, rapid, and very rapid.

LAND   The total natural and cultural environment within which production takes place; a broader term than soil. In addition to soil, its attributes include other physical conditions, such as mineral deposits, climate, and water supply; location in relation to centers of commerce, populations, and other land, the size of the individual tracts or holdings; and existing plant cover, works of improvement, and the like. Some use the terms loosely in other senses: as defined above but without the economic or cultural criteria; especially in the expression "natural land" as a synonym for "soil"; for the solid surface of the earth; and also for earthy surface formations, especially in the geomorphological expression "land form."

LAND CAPABILITY   The suitability of land for use without permanent damage. Land capability, as ordinarily used in the United States, is an expression of the effect of physical land conditions, including climate, on the total suitability for use without damage for crops that require regular tillage, for grazing, for woodland, and for wildlife. Land capability involves consideration of (1) the risks of land damage from erosion and other causes and (2) the difficulties in land use owing to physical land characteristics, including climate.

LAND CAPABILITY CLASSIFICATION   A grouping of kinds of soils into special units, subclasses, and classes according to their capability for intensive use and the treatments required for sustained use, prepared by the Soil Conservation Service, USDA.

LAND CAPABILITY MAP   A map showing land capability units, subclasses and classes, or a soil survey map colored to show land capability classes.

LAND CAPABILITY UNIT   Capability units provide more specific and detailed information for application to specific fields on a farm or ranch than the subclass of the land capability classification. A capability unit is a group of soils that are nearly alike in suitability for plant growth and responses to the same kinds of soil management.

LAND CLASSIFICATION   The arrangement of land units into various categories based on the properties of the land or its suitability for some particular purpose.

LAND FORM   A discernible natural landscape, such as a floodplain, stream terrace, plateau, valley, etc.

LEGUME   A member of the legume or pulse family, *Leguminosae*. One of the most important and widely distributed plant families. The fruit is a "legume" or pod that opens along two sutures when ripe. Flowers are usually papilionaceous (butterfly-like). Leaves are alternate, have stipules, and are usually compound. Includes many valuable food and forage species, such as the peas, beans, peanuts, cloves, alfalfas, sweet clovers, lespedezas, vetches, and kudzu. Practically all legumes are nitrogen-fixing plants.

LEVEL SPREADER   A shallow channel excavation at the outlet end of a diversion with a level section for the purpose of diffusing the diversion outflow.

LIME   Lime, from the strictly chemical standpoint, refers to only one compound, calcium oxide (CaO); however, the term "lime" is commonly used in agriculture to include a great variety of materials which are usually composed of the oxide, hydroxide, or carbonate of calcium or of calcium and magnesium. The most commonly used forms of agricultural lime are ground limestone (carbonates), hydrated lime (hydroxides), burnt lime (oxides), marl, and oyster shells.

LIME AGRICULTURAL   A soil amendment consisting principally of calcium carbonate but including magnesium carbonate and perhaps other materials, used to furnish calcium and magnesium carbonate and perhaps other materials, used to furnish calcium and magnesium as essential elements for the growth of plants and to neutralize soil acidity.

LIMING   The application of lime to land, primarily to reduce soil acidity and supply calcium for plant growth. Dolomitic limestone supplies both calcium and magnesium. May also improve soil structure, organic matter content, and nitrogen content of the soil by encouraging the growth of legumes and soil microorganisms. Liming an acid soil to pH value of about 6.5 is desirable for maintaining a high degree of availability of most of the nutrient elements required by plants.

LIQUEFACTION (*spontaneous liquefaction*)   The sudden large decrease of the shearing resistance of a cohesionless soil, caused by a collapse of the structure from shock or other type of strain and associated with a sudden but temporary increase in the pore-fluid pressure. It involves a temporary transformation of the material into a fluid mass.

LIQUID LIMIT   The moisture content at which the soil passes from a plastic to a liquid state. In engineering, a high liquid limit indicates that the soil has a high content of clay and low capacity for supporting loads.

LOAMY   Intermediate in texture and properties between fine-textured and coarse-textured soils.

LOOSE ROCK DAM   A dam built of rock without the use of mortar, a rubble dam. (See *Rock-Fill Dam.*)

MADE LAND   Areas filled with earth or earth and trash mixed, usually made by or under the control of man. A miscellaneous land type.

MANNING'S FORMULA *(hydraulics)*   A formula used to predict the velocity of water flow in an open channel or pipeline:

$$V = \left(\frac{1.486}{n}\right) r^{\frac{2}{3}} S^{\frac{1}{2}}$$

wherein V is the mean velocity of flow in feet per second; r is the hydraulic radius; S is the slope of the energy gradient or for assumed uniform flow the slope of the channel in feet per foot; and n is the roughness coefficient or retardance factor of the channel lining.

MEAN DEPTH *(hydraulics)*   Average depth; cross-sectional area of a stream or channel divided by its surface or top width.

MEAN VELOCITY   Average velocity obtained by dividing the flow rate (discharge) by the cross-sectional area for that given cross-section.

MEASURING WEIR   A shaped notch through which water flows are measured. Common shapes are rectangular, trapezoidal, and triangular.

MECHANICAL ANALYSIS   The analytical procedure by which soil particles are separated to determine the particle size distribution.

MECHANICAL PRACTICES   Soil and water conservation practices that primarily change the surface of the land or that store, convey, regulate, or dispose of runoff water without excessive erosion.

MOVABLE DAM   A movable barrier that may be opened in whole or in part, permitting control of the flow of water through or over the dam.

MUCK SOIL   1. An organic soil in which the organic matter is well decomposed (USA usage). 2. A soil containing 20 to 50 percent organic matter.

MULCH   A natural or artificial layer of plant residue or other materials, covering the land surface which conserves moisture, holds soil in place, aids in establishing plant cover, and minimizes temperature fluctuations.

NORMAL DEPTH   Depth of flow in an open conduit during uniform flow for the given conditions. (See *Uniform Flow.*)

OPEN DRAIN   Natural watercourse or constructed open channel that conveys drainage water.

OUTFALL   Point where water flows from a conduit, stream, or drain.

OUTLET   Point of water disposal from a stream, river, lake, tidewater, or artificial drain.

OUTLET CHANNEL   A waterway constructed or altered primarily to carry water from man-made structures, such as terraces, tile lines, and diversions.

OVERFALL   Abrupt change in stream channel elevation, the part of a dam or weir over which the water flows.

PEAK DISCHARGE   The maximum instantaneous flow from a given storm condition at a specific location.

PERMEABILITY   Capacity for transmitting a fluid. Measured by the rate at which a fluid of standard viscosity can move through material in a given interval of time under a given hydraulic gradient.

PERMEABILITY, SOIL   The quality of a soil horizon that enables water or air to move through it. The permeability of a soil may be limited by the presence of one nearly impermeable horizon even though the others are permeable.

PERMEABILITY   The rate at which water will move through a saturated soil. 1. *Slow—*

less than 0.120 inches per hour. 2. *Moderately slow*—0.120 to 0.63 inches per hour. 3. *Moderate*—0.63 to 2.0 inches per hour. 4. *Moderately rapid*—2.0 to 6.3 inches per hour. 5. *Rapid*—more than 6.3 inches per hour.

pH SOIL   A numerical measure of the acidity or hydrogen ion activity of a soil. The neutral point is pH 7.0. All pH values below 7.0 are acid and all above 7.0 are alkaline.

PIPE DROP   A circular conduit used to convey water down steep grades.

PLASTICITY INDEX   The numerical difference between the liquid limit and the plastic limit; the range of moisture content within which the soil remains plastic.

PLASTIC LIMIT   The moisture content at which a soil changes from a semisolid to a plastic state.

PLUNGE POOL   A device used to dissipate the energy of flowing water that may be constructed or made by the action of flowing. These facilities may be protected by various lining materials.

POOL   Section of stream deeper and usually wider than normal with appreciably slower current than immediate upstream or downstream areas and possessing adequate cover (sheer depth or physical condition) for protection of fish. Stream bottom usually a mixture of silt and coarse sand.

PRINCIPAL SPILLWAY   Generally constructed of permanent material and designed to regulate the normal water level, provide flood protection and/or reduce the frequency of operation of the emergency spillway.

RATIONAL FORMULA $Q = CIA$, where Q is the peak discharge measured in cubic feet per second, C is the runoff coefficient reflecting the ratio of runoff to rainfall, I is the rainfall intensity for the duration of the storm measured in inches per hour, and A is the area of the contributing drainage area measured in acres.

RILL   A small intermittent water course with steep sides, usually only a few inches deep and, hence, no obstacle to tillage operations.

RILL EROSION   See *Erosion*.

RIPRAP   Broken rock, cobbles, or boulders placed on earth surfaces, such as the face of a dam or the bank of a stream, for protection against the action of water (waves); also applied to brush or pole mattresses, or brush and stone, or other similar materials used for soil-erosion control.

RISER   The inlet portions of the drop-inlet spillway that extend vertically from the pipe conduit barrel to the water surface.

RIVER BASIN   The United States has been divided into 20 major water-resource regions (river basins).

ROADSIDE EROSION CONTROL   See *Highway Erosion Control*.

ROCK-FILL DAM   A dam composed of loose rock usually dumped in place, often with the upstream part constructed of hand-placed or derrick-placed rock and faced with rolled earth or with an impervious surface of concrete, timber, or steel.

RUNOFF *(hydraulics)*   That portion of the precipitation on a drainage area that is discharged from the area in stream channels. Types include runoff, groundwater runoff, or seepage.

SEDIMENT   Solid material, both mineral and organic, that is in suspension, is being transported, or has been moved from its site of origin by air, water, gravity, or ice and has come to rest on the earth's surface either above or below sea level.

SEDIMENT BASIN   A depression formed from the construction of a barrier or dam built at a suitable location to retain sediment and debris.

SEDIMENT DISCHARGE   The quantity of sediment, measured in dry weight or by volume, transported through a stream cross-section in a given time. Sediment discharge consists of both suspended load and bed load.

SEDIMENT GRADE SIZES   Measurements of sediment and soil particles that can be separated by screening. A committee on sedimentation of the National Research Council established a classification of textural grade sizes for standard use.

SEDIMENT LOAD   See *Sediment Discharge.*

SEDIMENT POOL   The reservoir space allotted to the accumulation of submerged sediment during the life of the structure.

SEEDBED   The soil prepared by natural or artificial means to promote the germination of seed and the growth of seedlings.

SEEPAGE   1. Water escaping through or emerging from the ground along an extensive line or surface as contrasted with a spring where the water emerges from a localized spot. 2. The process by which water percolates through the soil. 3. (percolation) The slow movement of gravitational water through the soil.

SILT   1. A soil separate consisting of particles between 0.05 and 0.002 millimeter in equivalent diameter. (See *Soil.*) 2. A soil textural class.

SILT LOAM   A soil textural class containing a large amount of silt and small quantities of sand and clay.

SILTY CLAY   A soil textural class containing a relatively large amount of silt and clay and a small amount of sand.

SILTY CLAY LOAM   A soil textural class containing a relatively large amount of silt, a lesser quantity of clay, and a still smaller quantity of sand.

SLOPE   Degree of deviation of a surface from the horizontal, usually expressed in percent or degrees.

SLOPE CHARACTERISTICS   Slopes may be characterized as concave (decrease in steepness in lower portion), uniform, or convex (increase in steepness at base). Erosion is strongly affected by shape, ranked in order of increasing erodibility from concave to uniform to convex.

SOIL   The unconsolidated mineral and organic material on the immediate surface of the earth that serves as a natural medium for the growth of land plants.

SOIL HORIZON   A layer of soil, approximately parallel to the surface, that has distinct characteristics produced by soil-forming factors.

SOIL PROFILE   A vertical section of the soil from the surface through all horizons, including *C* horizons.

SOLUM   The upper part of a soil profile, above the parent material, in which the processes of soil formation are active.

SPILLWAY   An open or closed channel, or both, used to convey excess water from a reservoir. It may contain gates, either manually or automatically controlled, to regulate the discharge of excess water.

STABILIZED CENTER SECTION   An area in the bottom of a grassed waterway protected by stone, asphalt, concrete, or other material to prevent erosion.

STABILIZED GRADE   The slope of a channel at which neither erosion nor deposition occurs.

STORM FREQUENCY   An expression or measure of how often a hydrologic event of a given size or magnitude should on an average be equaled or exceeded. The average should be based on a reasonable sample. (Expressed as 24 hour/year intervals.)

STREAMBANKS   The usual boundaries, not the flood boundaries, of a stream channel. Right and left banks are named facing downstream.

STREAM GAGING   The quantitative determination of stream flow using gages, current meters, weirs, or other measuring instruments at selected locations. (See *Gaging Station.*)

STREAM LOAD   Quantity of solid and dissolved material carried by a stream. (See *Sediment Discharge.*)

SUBSOIL   The *B* horizons of soils with distinct profiles. In soils with weak profile development, the subsoil can be defined as the soil below the plowed soil (or its equivalent of surface soil), in which roots normally grow. Although a common term, it cannot be defined accurately. It has been carried over from early days when "soil" was conceived only as the plowed soil and that under it as the "subsoil."

SUBWATERSHED   A watershed subdivision of unspecified size that forms a convenient natural unit.

TERRACE   An embankment or combination of an embankment and channel across a slope to control erosion by diverting or storing surface runoff instead of permitting it to flow uninterrupted down the slope.

TERRACE INTERVAL   Distance measured either vertically or horizontally between corresponding points on two adjacent terraces.

TERRACE OUTLET CHANNEL   Channel usually having a vegetative cover into which the flow from one or more terraces is discharged and conveyed from the field.

TERRACE SYSTEM   A series of terraces occupying a slope and discharging runoff into one or more outlet channels.

TILE, DRAIN   Pipe made of burned clay, concrete, or similar material, in short lengths, usually laid with open joints to collect and carry excess water from the soil.

TILE DRAINAGE   Land drainage by means of a series of tile lines laid at a specified depth and grade.

TOE DRAIN   A drainage system constructed in the downstream portion of an earth dam or levee to prevent excessive hydrostatic pressure.

TRASH RACK   A structural device used to prevent debris from entering a spillway or other hydraulic structure.

UNIFIED SOIL CLASSIFICATION SYSTEM (*engineering*)   A classification system based on the identification of soils according to their various properties that affect their use as construction materials.

UNIFORM FLOW   A state of steady flow when the mean velocity and cross-sectional area are equal at all sections of a reach.

UNIVERSAL SOIL-LOSS EQUATION   An equation used for the design of water-erosion control system: $A = RKLSPC$ wherein A = average annual soil loss in tons per acre per year; R = rainfall factor; K = soil erodibility factor; L = length of slope; S = percent of slope; P = conservation practice factor; and C = cropping and management factor. (T = soil loss tolerance value that has been assigned each soil, expressed $T/A/Year$.)

VEGETATIVE PROTECTION   Stabilization of erosive or sediment-producing areas by covering the soil with: 1. Permanent seeding, producing long-term vegetative cover. 2. Short-term seeding, producing temporary vegetative cover. 3. Sodding, producing areas covered with a turf of perennial sod-forming grass.

WATER CLASSIFICATION   Separation of water of an area into classes according to usage, such as domestic consumption, fisheries, recreation, industrial, agricultural, navigation, waste disposal, etc.

WATER CONSERVATION   The physical control, protection, management, and use of water resources in such a way as to maintain crop, grazing, and forest lands; vegetal cover; wildlife; and wildlife habitat for maximum sustained benefits to people, agriculture, industry, commerce, and other segments of the national economy.

WATER CONTROL (*soil and water conservation*)   The physical control of water by such measures as conservation practices on the land, channel improvement, and installation of structures for water retardation and sediment detention (does not refer to legal control or water rights as defined.)

WATER CUSHION   Pool of water maintained to absorb the impact of water flowing from an overfall structure.

WATER DEMAND   Water requirements for a particular purpose, such as irrigation, power, municipal supply, plant transportation, or storage.

WATER DISPOSAL SYSTEM   The complete system for removing excess water from land with minimum erosion. For sloping land, it may include a terrace system, terrace outlet channels, dams, and grassed waterways. For level land, it may include only surface drains or both surface and subsurface drains.

WATER QUALITY STANDARDS   Minimum requirements of purity of water for various uses; these standards are peculiar to each water classification as it applies to best usage.

WATER RESOURCES   The supply of groundwater and surface water in a given area.

WATERSHED AREA   All land and water within the confines of a drainage divide or a water problem area consisting in whole or in part of land needing drainage or irrigation.

WATERSHED LAG   Time from center of mass of effective rainfall to peak of hydrograph.

WATERSHED MANAGEMENT   Use, regulation, and treatment of water and land resources of a watershed to accomplish stated objectives.

WATERSHED PLANNING   Formulation of a plan to use and treat water and land resources.

WATERWAY   A natural course or constructed channel for the flow of water. (See *Grassed Waterway*.)

WEIR   Device for measuring or regulating the flow of water.

WEIR NOTCH   The opening in a weir for the passage of water.

Appendix 5

SAMPLE QUESTIONS

FROM A CLIENT'S STANDPOINT

During a land investigation I conducted in an eastern mountain area, my client presented me with a list of questions in his own words concerning the property I was investigating. I include this list in its original form (excluding county and proper names), because the wording in it may be helpful in clarifying certain parts of your investigation. I have also included my answers to the questions. The study concerned a 100-acre piece of mountain property.

SOIL

1. What is the nature of the soil?

The specific soils on your property will be determined by a free soil conservation study at your request. The general soils in the area of your property are Meyersville Loam, Manor Silt Loam, Chester Blenel Silt Loam, and Porters.

2. Does it perk?

From the examination by the local health official and from knowing the general types of soils in the area, the soil on your land should perk well enough to support at least one septic tank per two acres.

3. Can it be used for cultivation?

Yes. However, only the ridge tops and open areas could be used effectively. I would "guesstimate" that approximately 25 to 30 percent of the land could be efficiently cultivated.

4. Does the soil need fertilizer or lime?

Yes, the soil needs both lime and fertilizer. You can determine the amounts of each from a soil test conducted by the Agriculture Stabilization and Conservation Service. You need to provide them with a half Mason jar of soil from the farm.

5. Are there mineral deposits of any consequence?

A cursory examination indicates no evidence of any mineral deposits of any value on the property. The general area is also not noted for any consequential mineral deposits.

6. Suggestions for stopping the current erosion from cracks in land due to jeep trail.

Have a bulldozer fill and grade the eroded areas. Then lime the areas and seed them with a mixture of 50 percent rye (not rye grass) and 50 percent fescue.

TREES

1. How many years before selective cutting can begin?

Selective cutting should begin immediately in the thick growth areas. The trees are growing too closely together.

2. Value of timber now? Later?

The value of the timber now is negligible. Within 5 to 10 years, selective cutting could bring in $2,000 to $5,000 per year. Contact someone at a lumber company in town for an opinion.

3. Do you see any foreseeable problems due to disease?

I saw no evidence of disease in the trees. However, the Forest Service will give you a free appraisal of the condition of your trees.

4. How much is hardwood? Pine?

There are approximately equal amounts of hardwood and pine (mostly White Pine).

5. Would you suggest that trees be selectively cut for sale as lumber before lots are sold?

Only if they take away from the appearance of each lot.

6. What percentage of the land can be cleared and still offer an attractive development site? Value of timber?

There is no answer to your question, since each development buyer has his own idea of what is attractive.

WATER

1. Is water in streams good for drinking?

It is probably nontoxic; however, considering animal excrement, insects, etc., I would hesitate to drink it.

2. Where are the springs?

I did not examine the property closely enough to determine this.

3. Is there adequate water for development of the land into lots?

Yes.

4. Could there be a lake on this property? If so, where are the possible sites?

The only potential pond site is located in the stream at the bottom of the property.

ROADS

1. What would it cost to gravel one road for ourselves now (inside this property) from the bottom to the top of our land?

(The answer to this question was detailed in a separate report, which gave exact costs, and was acquired from the contractor.)

2. How wide should our access road be from the state road? How long?

For private use, 16 to 20 feet wide. For development use, 40 feet wide. It should be approximately 750 feet long before it starts up into your field.

3. What improvements would be necessary for this access road for development, i.e., rebuilding the bridge, paving, etc.?

For your private use the road could be graveled; for a development it would have to be paved. I would recommend a 48-inch-oval culvert rather than a bridge.

4. Can you give us an idea about what this might cost?

Please refer to Number 1 in this section.

OTHER

1. Using the topography of this land, what are the natural sites for lots for residential development?

(I provided the client with specific lot layouts.)

2. How large should each lot be?

Minimum size should be 10 acres.

3. How many lots?

Seven.

4. Where are the best places to situate the roads inside the property?

(I provided the client with specific lot layouts.)

5. What would be some alternatives to residential lots?

You could build apartments. Build a four-wheel drive obstacle course, put in a campground, put in a motorcycle motor-cross track, or lease the land for grazing or for cultivation.

6. What is the value of this land and its potential as an investment?

Here again, the answer to this question was detailed in a separate report.

7. Any idea when the city might grow out and annex this land?

It is doubtful that the town will annex this land in the near future.

8. How much should the taxes be?

Currently taxes run approximately $1/acre. This would increase to $10 to $15/acre for development lots.

9. How much should the grazing fee be?

A local farmer can better answer this question.

10. How can future erosion be controlled?

By not disturbing the land and by seeding where the land is disturbed.

11. What selling points or themes come to your mind as an aid in selling of this land from the standpoint of residential lots and alternative uses, too?

To sell it in large tracts of two to ten acres in size within the framework of a solidly funded membership association. Leave avenues open for the development of a central theme, such as horseback riding, tennis-club atmosphere, golf, etc.

12. What are some of the ordinances and restrictions governing residential development of this land in (County) or (Town)?

Please refer to the County Subdivision Ordinance attached to this report. (Such a report was attached.)

13. Could we attach the same restrictions to our lots as you did at your most recent development?

Yes.

14. What shape are the fences in on this land?

The boundary fences on the property seem to be in good order.

14a. How large a herd could graze this land?

No more than 12 head.

15. What is the tax situation like in the state?

(This answer depends on the state involved.)

16. Are there state income taxes?

(This answer depends on the state involved.)

17. Intangible taxes?

(This answer depends on the state involved.)

18. Would there be any tax advantages that could be provided by different uses of this land?

Yes, a variety of different situations which could best be described by your accountant.

Cattle farming, of course, would be one of the best. I would be happy to provide more details to you separately.

19. If farm land is developed, are there back taxes levied on the developer for changing the tax status of the land?

No.

20. Do I need any additional liability insurance for liabilities that could arise from this land (i.e., a child getting hurt on my property)?

You should get liability insurance for this land. Such insurance is most reasonable and should be available from the same people who currently cover your home.

21. How is this land zoned?

It is not.

22. Could it be developed for industrial purposes?

Yes.

23. Does the land drain well?

Yes.

24. What type of free services does the government offer a farm, i.e., help with land and soil conservation, tree planting, etc.?

I have stated several in this report. Free trees are given out from time to time by the State Forest Service.

25. Can you foresee any liabilities or problems from construction of roads and buildings in this area?

No.

26. To develop residential lots in this area, what type of compliance is required by developers, i.e., paved roads or gravel, sewage facilities, electrical hook-up, garbage removal?

Please refer to the subdivision ordinance which is attached. Generally you must put in paved roads to state specifications, institute a soil drainage and erosion plan, and provide a main power line.

27. Can you estimate these costs?

28. Can you estimate development costs, number of lots, price for individual lots?

29. Estimation of potential profits.

(Here again, the answers to these questions were detailed in a separate report.)

INDEX